POWERFUL VOCABULARY FOR READING SUCCESS

STUDENT'S EDITION
GRADE 4

Dr. Cathy Collins Block
Professor of Education
Texas Christian University
and Member, Board of Directors
International Reading Association (2002-2005)

Dr. John N. Mangieri
Director
Institute for Literacy Enhancement

■ SCHOLASTIC

New York ✸ Toronto ✸ London ✸ Auckland ✸ Sydney
Mexico City ✸ New Delhi ✸ Hong Kong ✸ Buenos Aires

ISBN: 0-439-64051-2

Cover design by James Sarfati
Interior design by Grafica, Inc.
Interior Illustrations by Jeff Shelly and Teresa Southwell

TABLE OF CONTENTS

CHAPTER 1

CHAPTER 2

TABLE OF CONTENTS

CHAPTER 3

CHAPTER 4

CHAPTER 1

Context Clues

Read Words in Context

Word Learning Tip!

A **noun** is a word that names a person, place, or thing. A noun often appears before a verb and may have the word *a*, *an*, or *the* in front of it. A noun may be singular or it may be a plural, ending in –*s*, –*es*, or –*ies*. You can use these clues—and ask whether the word names a person, place, or thing—to determine if an unknown word is a noun.

Vocabulary Building Strategy

Use Context Clues You can find the meaning of nouns you don't know by using the context. Put together the meanings of all the words around an unknown word. This will help you understand a noun's meaning.

The After-School Garden

Danica was excited. The school **auditorium** was packed full of people. Students and teachers sat in rows facing the stage. The principal, Mrs. Yee, introduced the **speaker**.

Mr. Williams spoke in a friendly **manner** to the students. He said that students would grow vegetables on the school **property**. It was a piece of land next to the playground. The gardeners would gain **knowledge** about how to take care of plants.

This was a great **opportunity** for students to enjoy themselves, learn about plants, and grow some delicious, fresh vegetables to bring home. The **quality** would be very high.

Danica went home to her family's **apartment** in the building on Worth Street. She had an **agreement** for her parents to sign. This piece of paper said they would let Danica work on the garden after school. They were happy to sign the agreement. Signing it wasn't an **issue**, or hard decision, for them.

Seeing all the students outside on their knees in the garden was a **spectacle** to behold—a truly remarkable sight! They worked with great care, planting tomatoes, beans, carrots, squash, and lettuce in neat rows. The teachers watched the students' careful **movements** as they tried not to step on any of the new plants just coming up.

The students soon learned that the **basis** of gardening is to keep plants healthy. Gardeners water plants, keep them free of bugs, and keep away animals that might eat them.

When the vegetables ripened, they were in great **condition**. The kids had more than enough to take home. They set up a stand at the local fire **station** to sell the extra vegetables.

Connect Words and Meanings

agreement	basis	knowledge	opportunity	speaker
apartment	condition	manner	property	spectacle
auditorium	issue	movement	quality	station

Directions Read the numbered words. Then find the definition of each word. Write the letter of the definition in the blank next to the word. You may use the glossary to help you.

Word	Definition
1. _____ agreement	**A.** information or know-how and skill
2. _____ auditorium	**B.** an exciting or remarkable sight or event
3. _____ basis	**C.** two people sign a paper to say they will do something
4. _____ issue	**D.** a chance to do something
5. _____ knowledge	**E.** buildings, land, and other things belonging to someone
6. _____ manner	**F.** a large room where people gather for meetings, plays, concerts, and other events
7. _____ opportunity	**G.** the way someone acts or does something
8. _____ property	**H.** the idea or reason behind something
9. _____ quality	**I.** topic to think about or decide on
10. _____ spectacle	**J.** the fineness or worth of something

(continued on next page)

Connect More Words and Meanings

agreement	basis	knowledge	opportunity	speaker
apartment	condition	manner	property	spectacle
auditorium	issue	movement	quality	station

Directions Read the definition above the squares. Write in the word from the vocabulary list that fits the definition. Then put together the letters in the numbered squares to spell out the name of a plant that Danica and her friends grew in their garden. (Put the letters in numerical order.) You may use the glossary to help you.

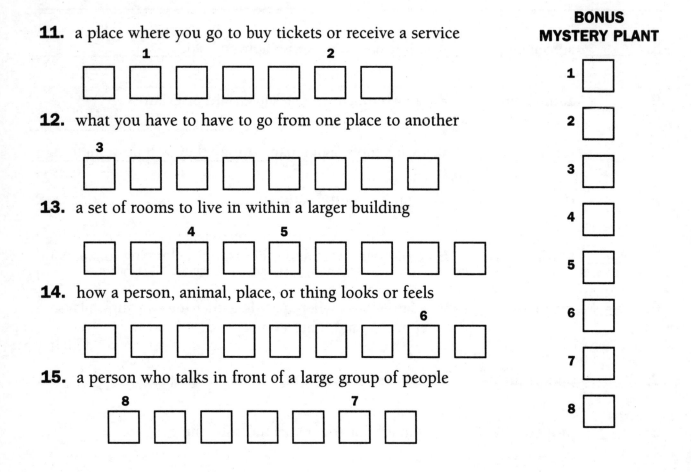

BONUS MYSTERY PLANT

11. a place where you go to buy tickets or receive a service

12. what you have to have to go from one place to another

13. a set of rooms to live in within a larger building

14. how a person, animal, place, or thing looks or feels

15. a person who talks in front of a large group of people

. . . .

⭐ **Sentence Round Robin** Work with a partner to continue a story. Your first sentence is: *It was the opportunity of a lifetime.* On a separate sheet of paper, write the next sentence for the story. Use one of your vocabulary words. Then give the paper to your partner so that your partner can write the third sentence using another vocabulary word. See how long you can keep the story going.

Use Words in Context

agreement	basis	knowledge	opportunity	speaker
apartment	condition	manner	property	spectacle
auditorium	issue	movement	quality	station

Directions Use your vocabulary words to write a sentence answering each question below.

1. If you had the **opportunity** to take a trip, where would you go? _____

_____

2. About what topic would you like to have more **knowledge**? _____

_____

3. What would you like to learn about from a **speaker**? _____

_____

4. What activity takes place in the school **auditorium**? _____

_____

5. What kind of **spectacle** would you like to be in: a parade or a show? Tell why.

_____

6. Why must your parents sign an **agreement** before you can join an after-school activity?

_____

7. What is an **issue** you would have to think about before you joined an after-school

activity? _____

8. How does your school want students to behave on school **property**?

_____

 Tell About It Imagine you are making a movie about yourself. Create a storyboard showing two hours in a day in your life after school. Write as many frames as you like.

Put Words Into Action

agreement	basis	knowledge	opportunity	speaker
apartment	condition	manner	property	spectacle
auditorium	issue	movement	quality	station

Directions The word meaning map below has questions for you to answer about the word *spectacle*. Fill in the answers in the boxes.

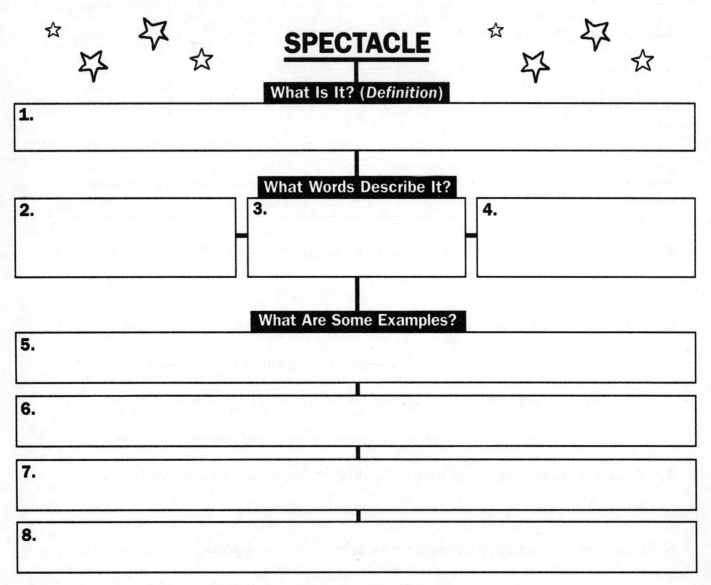

SPECTACLE

What Is It? (Definition)

1.

What Words Describe It?

2.

3.

4.

What Are Some Examples?

5.

6.

7.

8.

 Make Word Meaning Maps Work in a group of five students. Make word meaning maps for five vocabulary nouns. After your group is finished, discuss each word map.

Review and Extend

agreement	basis	knowledge	opportunity	speaker
apartment	condition	manner	property	spectacle
auditorium	issue	movement	quality	station

Learn More! A noun can be either **singular** or **plural**. A **singular noun** names one person, place, or thing. A **plural noun** names more than one.

Singular Noun	What to Do to Make Plural	Plural Noun
agreement	Add –s at end for most nouns	agreements
wish	If a noun ends in –s, –sh, –ch, –z, or –x, add –es	wishes
property	If a noun ends in a consonant and –y, change the –y to –i and add –es	properties

Directions Choose the right vocabulary word from the box to fit in the blank. A context clue is printed in boldface type. Add the ending –s or –es to the word you chose. Write your answer on the blank. In the vocabulary box, put a check next to each word you use.

1. Many students look for **chances** to sing, dance, or play an instrument. In school shows, there are many _____ to do these things.

2. School shows are held in **the room set aside for plays and concerts.** Most _____ have stages with special lighting and a curtain.

3. Parents have to **sign papers** so that students can perform in the school shows. These _____ say that students can stay after school to practice.

4. The dance teacher taught the boys and girls some **neat steps**. The group's _____ became smoother the more they practiced.

5. School shows are **exciting and dramatic events**. The many talented performers make these _____ fun to watch.

 Add to Your Personal Word List Write the plurals for the vocabulary words that you didn't check. Do not write plurals for *knowledge* and *basis*.

1 Nouns to Know

Check Your Mastery

Directions Answer each of the following questions with a sentence using the word in boldface. Write your sentences on the blanks.

1. Why might it be fun to live in a building with many **apartments**? _____

_____

2. What are three different kinds of **stations** you might find in a city? _____

_____

3. Why is it better for two people to sign an **agreement** instead of just saying they will do

something? _____

_____

4. What decisions might a general make about the **movement** of troops? _____

_____

5. Why is it important to keep a bike in good **condition**? _____

_____

Directions Read each item below. Circle the letter of the best choice to complete each sentence.

6. A good place to see a class play is in the school _____.
   A. manner   **B.** basis   **C.** auditorium   **D.** property

7. If a coat is poorly made, it is not of good _____.
   A. quality   **B.** issue   **C.** spectacle   **D.** speaker

8. If you need answers to questions, you look for someone who has a lot of _____.
   A. agreement   **B.** knowledge   **C.** opportunity   **D.** condition

9. If you need someone to give a talk at a meeting, you try to find a _____.
   A. speaker   **B.** quality   **C.** spectacle   **D.** knowledge

10. Someone who likes to travel would look for a job that offers this _____.
   A. basis   **B.** quality   **C.** manner   **D.** opportunity

Read Words in Context

READ!

Racers on Four Paws

Every March, teams of sled dogs **compete** in a special race called the Iditarod [I-*dit*-er-ohd]. They pull a sled over more than a thousand miles of ice and snow across Alaska from Anchorage to Nome. The fastest team wins.

Winning depends on having a good team of dogs. Most drivers **prefer** huskies, since this breed of dog has a lot of energy. A race as hard as the Iditarod would **exhaust** weaker dogs.

The dogs and their human drivers train all year. They need to **maintain** good health and fitness so that they're ready for this difficult race.

The dog at the head of the team is the lead dog. During the race, drivers **assume** that their lead dog will follow their commands right away. If the lead dog **hesitates**, the other dogs will be confused. They might become upset or **annoyed**.

Drivers are careful not to **endanger** the dogs. They look for dangerous patches of ice. They watch the team for signs of trouble. Limping or a drooping head may **indicate** that a dog is injured or sick. The driver must not **neglect** a dog that needs help.

There are several rest stops along the way. At a rest stop, the driver will **release** the dogs from their harnesses. The driver and dogs **seize** the opportunity to eat and rest. The resting time **relieves** the lead dog from its job for a while.

After this rest, the team gets back to the race and **advances** over the icy trail. The first teams may reach the finish line in about ten days.

Dog-sled racing **fascinates** many people. They become fans of one driver and team and are there every year to cheer them on!

Vocabulary Words

advance	indicate
annoy	maintain
assume	neglect
compete	prefer
endanger	release
exhaust	relieve
fascinate	seize
hesitate	

Word Learning Tip!

A **verb** is a word that shows actions or feelings. Often a verb comes right after a noun or pronoun. Sometimes you can spot a verb because it ends in –s, –ed, or –ing. Sometimes a verb has a helping word such as *may, can, could, shall, should, will,* or *would* in front of it. You can use these clues to learn new words.

Vocabulary Building Strategy

Use Context Clues When you come across a verb you do not know, look at the context. Often, you will find clues that help you understand what someone or something is doing or feeling. These clues will help you determine the meaning of the unfamiliar verb.

Connect Words and Meanings

advance	compete	fascinate	maintain	release
annoy	endanger	hesitate	neglect	relieve
assume	exhaust	indicate	prefer	seize

Directions Read each definition below. Circle the word that matches each definition. You may use the glossary to help you.

1. to take away a problem or chore or to ease someone's trouble or pain

    compete   neglect   relieve

2. to make someone feel angry or upset or lose patience

    seize   annoy   prefer

3. to make very tired

    neglect   compete   exhaust

4. to like one thing better than another

    advance   assume   prefer

5. to suppose that something is true or will happen without checking it

    neglect   assume   relieve

6. to free something or someone

    exhaust   release   advance

7. to try hard to do better than others at a task or in a race or other contest

    compete   neglect   exhaust

8. to show or point out something

    hesitate   maintain   indicate

9. to move forward toward a goal

    relieve   assume   advance

10. to attract and hold someone's attention

    prefer   fascinate   annoy

(continued on next page)

Connect More Words and Meanings

advance	compete	fascinate	maintain	release
annoy	endanger	hesitate	neglect	relieve
assume	exhaust	indicate	prefer	seize

Directions Continue the activity. Read each definition below. Circle the word that matches each definition. You may use the glossary to help you.

11. to keep something in good condition or continue to do something

maintain   **indicate**   **hesitate**

12. to grab or take hold of something quickly or suddenly

relieve   **annoy**   **seize**

13. to put in a dangerous or risky situation

maintain   **endanger**   **hesitate**

14. to pause before you do something, or to not do something right away

indicate   **hesitate**   **maintain**

15. to fail to take care of someone or something

neglect   **advance**   **relieve**

BONUS Write three sentences using three different vocabulary words.

16. _____

_____

17. _____

_____

18. _____

_____

⭐ **Use Verbs to Ask and Answer Riddles** Write "What Am I?" riddles to stump your classmates. Select a person or thing. Then write statements that tell what this person or thing does. For example: *I help sailors. I indicate what way to go in the dark. What am I?* (Answer: A lighthouse) Use five vocabulary words and five new verbs in your riddles.

Use Words in Context

advance	compete	fascinate	maintain	release
annoy	endanger	hesitate	neglect	relieve
assume	exhaust	indicate	prefer	seize

Directions Bianca is writing a report about a long race called a marathon. Help her rewrite her sentences. Cross out the words in boldface. Replace them with the right vocabulary word. Write the word on the blank.

1. Long races **hold the attention of** fans for hours. _____

2. Many fans **like much better** to watch these races in person than to watch them on television. _____

3. Hundreds of racers **go against one another** for the glory of winning the marathon.

   _____

4. A racer must **keep up** a comfortable speed in order not to get too tired.

   _____

5. Racers should be careful not to **get too tired** themselves. _____

6. A racer cannot **fail to take care of** a problem when he or she is racing.

   _____

7. They must wear the right running shoes to **take away the problems of** their tired feet.

   _____

8. If racers run with a hurt leg or foot, they **risk danger to** themselves.

   _____

9. The best racers **move ahead** toward the finish line. _____

10. One racer may **grab or take hold of** the opportunity to pull ahead of the others and win.

   _____

⭐ **Write a Tall Tale** Make up a tall tale about a race or competition. Your race doesn't have to be between two people. It could be about two animals or even two things, for instance. Try to make your tale as exaggerated and outlandish as you can. Use at least five vocabulary words and two new verbs in your tale.

Put Words Into Action

advance	compete	fascinate	maintain	release
annoy	endanger	hesitate	neglect	relieve
assume	exhaust	indicate	prefer	seize

Directions Some verbs show physical activity. Others show mental activity, or actions that go on entirely in your mind. Think about each vocabulary word. Sort the words into these two categories: "Physical Activities" and "Mental Activities," Some words may fit in both categories if the action is physical but is also something that can go on in your head. List those words under "Both."

PHYSICAL ACTIVITIES

1. _____
2. _____
3. _____
4. _____
5. _____
6. _____
7. _____

MENTAL ACTIVITIES

8. _____
9. _____
10. _____

BOTH

11. _____
12. _____
13. _____
14. _____
15. _____

Illustrate Words Look at your list of words under Physical Activities. Choose five of them. For each, write the word and its definition on one side of a piece of paper. Find a photograph in a magazine or newspaper or draw a picture to illustrate each word. Put the illustration on the reverse side.

Review and Extend

advance	compete	fascinate	maintain	release
annoy	endanger	hesitate	neglect	relieve
assume	exhaust	indicate	prefer	seize

Learn More! The **ending** of a verb tells when something happens. This is called the **tense**.

Present Tense	Past Tense	Ongoing Action
he jumps	he jumped	he is jumping
she imagines	she imagined	she is imagining

Directions Read each pair of sentences. Then fill in the blank with the correct verb from the vocabulary list. Be sure to put the verb in the correct tense. You may have to add one of these endings to the verb: –s, –ed, –ing. If the verb ends in –e, drop the –e before adding –ed or –ing.

1. Two children raced down the street. The faster one _____

the lead when the other tripped.

2. Cala likes to read biographies of famous athletes. She _____

them to any other kind of book.

3. The police officer is pointing at our car. She is _____

that we must wait until the racers pass.

4. Jarret _____ the balloons when the race was over.

They flew up into the sky.

5. One runner did not act quickly enough. He _____

at the starting line.

 **Play the Definitions Game** Here are the directions for playing the definitions game: Work with a group of five students. Choose three vocabulary words. Create both correct and incorrect definitions to stump your classmates. Take a piece of paper and cut it in half. Write one verb and its definition on one piece. Write the verb and an incorrect definition on the other piece. Do this for each of your three words. Then the group puts all the slips of paper in a pile in the center of the table. Everyone takes a turn and selects a slip. Can each person identify if the verb is matched with the correct definition?

Check Your Mastery

Directions Choose the correct word to fit in each sentence from the three that appear in the parentheses. Write it on the blank.

1. Two people are on a game show. They are _____
(*competing, fascinating, releasing*) for a prize.

2. A red traffic light _____ (*neglects, exhausts, indicates*) "stop."

3. The boy paused for a short time before answering the question. He _____
(*advanced, hesitated, released*) until he was sure of the answer.

4. Don't be too sure that your facts are correct. I _____
(*assumed, preferred, relieved*) that, but I was wrong.

5. Jake _____ (*competed, assumed, seized*) the ball and ran for the finish line.

Directions In the left-hand column are ten vocabulary words. In the right-hand column are ten situations. Match each situation with a verb you could use to describe it. Write the letter of the situation in the blank by the word.

	Words		Situations
_____	**6.** exhaust	**A.**	Paint fumes may put painters at risk so they wear masks.
_____	**7.** neglect	**B.**	The players move up to the next level.
_____	**8.** prefer	**C.**	The workers let the bird caught in the screen go.
_____	**9.** relieve	**D.**	Mariah is worn out from climbing up the mountain.
_____	**10.** endanger	**E.**	Alex likes strawberries better than apples.
_____	**11.** fascinate	**F.**	The flies buzzed around his head.
_____	**12.** advance	**G.**	Harry let his bicycle rust.
_____	**13.** annoy	**H.**	Karim takes the place of a tired player.
_____	**14.** maintain	**I.**	Lucinda keeps her skates in good condition.
_____	**15.** release	**J.**	The clowns hold everyone's attention.

Read Words in Context

Vocabulary Words

abandon	impress
accuse	improve
budge	intend
commit	involve
damage	loosen
discover	nudge
explode	succeed
forgive	

Word Learning Tip!

A **verb** shows an action or a feeling. A complete sentence has both a subject and a verb. The subject tells who is doing the action or having the feeling. The subject and verb in a sentence agree in number, or match.

Vocabulary Building Strategy

Use Context Clues You can find the meaning of verbs you don't know by using context clues. Look for words you know that are near the unknown word. Also look at the whole passage. Using context clues can help you determine a verb's meaning.

 READ!

The Case of the Missing Tuna

Like most cats, I like my comfort. Usually, I do not **budge** from my bed before noon. Normally, nothing can move me to get up early, but today a strange feeling led me to **abandon** my soft cushion.

Never in my eight years of life have I felt such pangs. At first, I thought my stomach would **explode**, or burst. Perhaps I felt this way because I had licked up that spilled salt the night before. I hadn't **intended** to, but I couldn't resist when I saw it there.

I must **impress** upon you that I don't usually give in to temptation. But you'll have to **forgive** me. No one is perfect, not even me.

Then I realized that this strange feeling didn't **involve** being too full. It came from being hungry. I walked over to my food bowl, but what I saw there didn't **improve** the situation. It was empty.

In the old days, my bowl was always kept full. But then the veterinarian **discovered** this fact: When she found out that I could snack whenever I wanted, she **accused** me of eating too much. The unfairness of it all! Now I can no longer get a decent bellyful at all hours.

Then I saw a bowl of tuna sitting on the kitchen counter. I guess someone was about to make lunch. Could these aging muscles do it? Could I **succeed** in making the jump? I sprang with all my might and landed on the counter. I **nudged** the bowl, which fell to the floor. Immediately I followed, leaping down. The bowl wasn't **damaged** or hurt. I started eating quickly, gobbling up the delicious chunks. Some of the tuna was stuck to the sides, so I used my paws to **loosen** the stuck chunks. What a satisfying meal. Today, I **committed** my first crime and became a cat burglar.

Connect Words and Meanings

abandon	commit	explode	improve	loosen
accuse	damage	forgive	intend	nudge
budge	discover	impress	involve	succeed

Directions Read each definition clue below. Write the vocabulary word that fits each meaning in the crossword puzzle. You may use the glossary to help you.

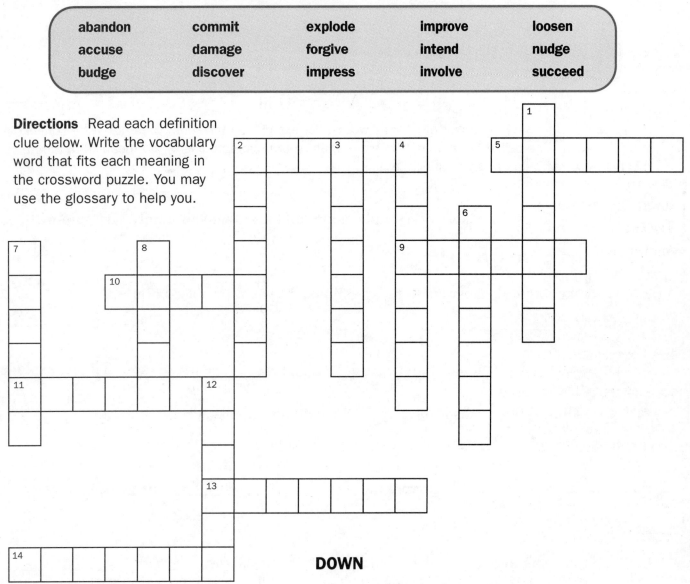

ACROSS

2. to mean to do something

5. to make something less tight

9. to do something wrong or not lawful

10. to move something

11. to get what you want

13. to leave forever

14. to include someone or something as a necessary part

DOWN

1. to pardon or to stop blaming someone

2. to make someone think highly of you or to affect strongly

3. to blow apart

4. to find something

6. to get better at something or to make something better

7. to say someone has done something wrong

8. to give someone or something a small push

12. to harm something

Connect More Words and Meanings

abandon	commit	explode	improve	loosen
accuse	damage	forgive	intend	nudge
budge	discover	impress	involve	succeed

Directions A "hink pink" is a pair of rhyming words. For example, a tiny room you enter after coming in the door could be called a "small hall." Demonstrate your understanding of the meaning of the vocabulary words below by completing the hink pinks.

1. Everyone loves the baker's cakes and cookies and says that she simply can't **improve** her _____ treats.

2. When he forgot the answers to the questions, his friends **accused** him of having a _____ drain.

3. I'm so angry that you had better _____ clear of me or I'll just **explode**.

4. Since all his phone calls **involved** complaining, his parents accused him of having a _____ phone.

5. In the river, the police **discovered** the _____ barge used to carry stolen goods.

6. The thief **committed** a crime by taking money from the cash _____.

7. "I **forgive** you. I know you didn't mean it," said Aunt Priscilla. "You're so silly. You're just a _____ billy."

8. **Impress** your friends. Ask your parents if you can have a tray to create a tray _____ to slide down the hill in the snow.

 **Favorite Recipe Stories** In your personal word journal, write a paragraph about a favorite recipe that a family member or someone else cooks for you. Try to include why you like this recipe. Is this food cooked often or only on special occasions? Does it have any special ingredients? Use at least two vocabulary words and two new verbs.

Use Words in Context

abandon	commit	explode	improve	loosen
accuse	damage	forgive	intend	nudge
budge	discover	impress	involve	succeed

Directions Read each sentence below. Write the word that best fits in the blank.

1. Fernando and I start a cooking club. Most meetings _____ (*discover, impress, involve*) learning how to cook a different cookie recipe.

2. The club likes to cook oatmeal cookies. We _____ (*improve, forgive, abandon*) the recipe every time we bake them.

3. Armando wanted to _____ (*nudge, succeed, impress*) his friends with a special treat, so we baked delicious ginger cookies.

4. Jenna was very happy to _____ (*discover, accuse, commit*) a lemon cookie recipe in an old cookbook in the attic.

5. Charlene refuses to join the club. At first, she won't _____ (*nudge, budge, forgive*). Then she decides that she'll try one meeting.

6. Most of the club members _____ (*impress, succeed, damage*) in learning how to make three cookie recipes.

7. Alba _____ (*nudges, forgives, abandons*) Jake to ask him a question: "How much sugar do we need?"

8. Angela tries a recipe in which she has to roll out dough, but she has to _____ (*loosen, abandon, explode*) it from the bowl first. The cookie dough falls apart!

9. Jason does not _____ (*intend, involve, commit*) to keep making the same mistake of burning the cookies.

10. Everyone is willing to _____ (*forgive, explode, accuse*) any cooking mistake if the cookies taste good!

....

Make a Flyer Selling cookies is a good way to raise money. Use a sheet of paper to design and write a flyer that tells about the club's yearly cookie fair. Include a description of the fair and when and where it will take place. Make up some original names for the cookies that will be sold. Use several vocabulary words along with one or two new verbs.

3 **More Verbs to Know**

Put Words Into Action

abandon	commit	explode	improve	loosen
accuse	damage	forgive	intend	nudge
budge	discover	impress	involve	succeed

Directions Look at each picture and read the definition. Choose the word from the vocabulary list that fits the definition. Write it in the blank. Then write a sentence using the word.

Definition: to move something out of position

1. Word: _____

2. My Sentence: _____

Definition: to find something by chance

3. Word: _____

4. My Sentence: _____

Definition: to give someone a small push

5. Word: _____

6. My Sentence: _____

Definition: to make someone think highly of you

7. Word: _____

8. My Sentence: _____

⭐ **Create a Comic Strip** Work with a partner. Use a sheet of paper to draw a comic strip about a funny food detective. Brainstorm with your partner. Decide what food mystery the detective has to solve and how the detective solves it. Use some of your vocabulary words in the cartoon speech bubbles that you create for words that the detective speaks.

Review and Extend

abandon	commit	explode	improve	loosen
accuse	damage	forgive	intend	nudge
budge	discover	impress	Involve	succeed

Learn More! A complete sentence should have a subject and a verb. The subject and verb must **agree**, or match. If the subject is **singular** (only one), the verb must be singular. If the subject is **plural** (more than one), the verb must be plural.

In the present tense, add –s or –es to verbs when the subject is a singular noun or the pronouns are *he, she,* or *it.* Do not add an –s or –es when the subject is a plural noun or if the pronouns are *we, you,* or *they.*

Present Tense of Verb	
Singular	**Plural**
The girl eats.	The girl and boy eat.
She eats.	They eat.

Directions Read each sentence below. First, choose the verb that best fits in each sentence. Then, in the blank, write the verb in the present tense in its singular or plural form. Make sure that the subject and the verb agree.

1. Lionel and Max _____ (*abandon, forgive, impress*) their sister for eating all the popcorn.

2. Fiona tries to follow the recipe for making tacos and she _____ (*budge, damage, succeed*).

3. Iliana _____ (*commit, accuse, improve*) Hector of taking the last cookie from the cookie jar.

4. Tarik and Tony _____ (*intend, loosen, involve*) to learn how to cook pizza someday.

5. Lucy _____ (*nudge, accuse, discover*) Teddy to remind him to thank Mrs. James for the taco.

★ **Create a Word Web** Write the following category in the center circle of a word web: Things That Won't Budge. Then brainstorm to come up with as many words as you can to fit this category. Write them in the empty circles.

Check Your Mastery

Directions Read each item below. Circle the letter of the verb that best fits the meaning.

1. If you want a friend to change his mind, you might try to get him to do this.

   A. accuse   **B.** budge   **C.** damage

2. A person who wants to be your friend might try to do this.

   A. impress you   **B.** involve you   **C.** abandon you

3. If you receive an invitation to a party, you probably do this.

   A. forgive someone   **B.** explode with anger   **C.** intend to go

4. If you are not doing well in a subject, you might study hard so that your grades would do this.

   A. improve   **B.** impress   **C.** succeed

5. Firefighters might do this if they felt they couldn't save a building.

   A. commit it   **B.** damage it   **C.** abandon it

Directions Choose a vocabulary word to complete each sentence below. Write the word in the blank.

6. A scientist _____ (*abandons, succeeds, discovers*) a cure for a sickness. His discovery helps many people.

7. After eating a big meal, Damien _____ (*loosens, damages, improves*) his belt. The belt feels too tight.

8. Brian _____ (*impresses, nudges, explodes*) his friend Jesse with his elbow. He wants to get Jesse's attention.

9. When the fireworks _____ (*explode, damage, budge*), they make beautiful designs in the sky.

10. Tara _____ (*accuses, forgives, intends*) Jake for ruining her favorite CD because she knows he feels bad.

Read Words in Context

READ!

A Day in the Life of the Taino

*Long ago, the Taino [**Tah**-ee-no] people lived on some of the islands in the Caribbean Sea. They lived on what are now Puerto Rico, Cuba, Haiti, and the Dominican Republic. This story shows what the life of these Indians was like more than five hundred years ago.*

A Taino woman **awoke** at dawn. She **rose** early and got up from her sleeping hammock. This hanging bed **swung** between two wooden posts inside her house. Then she prepared breakfast for her family. She took some corn flour from a basket. The flour had been **ground** from corn that she grew herself. She mixed the flour with water and made corn cakes.

Her husband and children **sprang** from their hammocks. They jumped up eager to begin the day. The children **left** the house to search for wood for the cooking fire. After they **found** the wood and **brought** it back to the house, she cooked the corn cakes over the fire. After the flat cakes were baked, she **spread** them out on a mat. Each member of the family **tore** off a piece of corn cake to **bite** into.

During the day, the Taino mother and children took care of their corn, yams, and other plants. One child found a snakeskin in the field—the outer skin that a snake had **shed**.

The father joined a hunting party looking for iguanas and sea turtles. These hunters **understood** the habits of the animals they hunted. They knew where to find them. The hunters **crept** up behind the animals and caught them.

The sons had **become** expert fishermen. Sometimes they caught fish with their hands, sometimes they used nets, and sometimes they used lines. Today, they were lucky. They brought home several fish to cook for dinner.

Vocabulary Words

- awake/awoke/awoken
- become/became/become
- bite/bit/bitten
- bring/brought/brought
- creep/crept/crept
- find/found/found
- grind/ground/ground
- leave/left/left
- rise/rose/risen
- shed/shed/shed
- spread/spread/spread
- spring/sprang/sprung
- swing/swung/swung
- tear/tore/torn
- understand/understood/ understood

Word Learning Tip!

A **verb** is a word that describes an action or a state of being. It usually is the word right after the noun. Irregular verbs like the ones in this lesson don't form the past tense by adding *-d* or *-ed*.

Vocabulary Building Strategy

Use Context Clues You can find the meaning of verbs you don't know by using the context. Put together the meanings of all the words around an unknown word. Also look at the tense of the verb. This will help you determine a verb's meaning.

4 Irregular Verbs to Know

Connect Words and Meanings

awake/awoke/awoken	find/found/found	spread/spread/spread
become/became/become	grind/ground/ground	spring/sprang/sprung
bite/bit/bitten	leave/left/left	swing/swung/swung
bring/brought/brought	rise/rose/risen	tear/tore/torn
creep/crept/crept	shed/shed/shed	understand/understood/understood

Directions Find the vocabulary word that best fits each meaning. Write it in the blank next to the definition. Use only the present-tense form of the verb (*awake*, *become*, and so on). You may use the glossary to help you.

_____ **1.** to discover or come across something

_____ **2.** to take someone or something with you; to carry

_____ **3.** to go away from or out of

_____ **4.** to cover a surface with something; to unfold or stretch out

_____ **5.** to get up from sleep

_____ **6.** to rip or pull apart; to make an opening

_____ **7.** to know what something means or how it works

_____ **8.** to close your teeth around something; to cut with your teeth

_____ **9.** to move back and forth, especially on a hinge

_____ **10.** to start to be

(continued on next page)

Connect More Words and Meanings

awake/awoke/awoken find/found/found spread/spread/spread

become/became/become grind/ground/ground spring/sprang/sprung

bite/bit/bitten leave/left/left swing/swung/swung

bring/brought/brought rise/rose/risen tear/tore/torn

creep/crept/crept shed/shed/shed understand/understood/
understood

Directions Read each word and the meanings below it. Circle the letter of the meaning that defines the word. You may use the glossary to help you.

11. creep
- **A.** move slowly and quietly
- **B.** move quickly and forcefully
- **C.** move up and down

12. grind
- **A.** work hard
- **B.** crush something into a powder
- **C.** make music

13. rise
- **A.** have
- **B.** go up or get up
- **C.** sing

14. shed
- **A.** cover something
- **B.** put away
- **C.** let something fall or drop off; give off

15. spring
- **A.** jump suddenly; leap
- **B.** walk up stairs
- **C.** go back and forth over and over again

16. swing
- **A.** move back and forth
- **B.** discover something
- **C.** take something back

17. leave
- **A.** cut apart
- **B.** get out of bed
- **C.** go away from

18. spread
- **A.** unfold or stretch out
- **B.** crush something into a powder
- **C.** give off

Write Now and Long-Ago Stories Work with a partner to brainstorm about how the morning activities of a family today compares with those of a Taino family of long ago. Think about how the activities are similar and how they are different. Then write a paragraph in your journal telling about the comparisons. Try to use at least four vocabulary words and four new verbs.

Use Words in Context

awake/awoke/awoken	find/found/found	spread/spread/spread
become/became/become	grind/ground/ground	spring/sprang/sprung
bite/bit/bitten	leave/left/left	swing/swung/swung
bring/brought/brought	rise/rose/risen	tear/tore/torn
creep/crept/crept	shed/shed/shed	understand/understood/ understood

Directions Answer each question below by writing a sentence using the vocabulary word in boldface. Write your sentence with the vocabulary word on the blank line.

1. What can you do with a piece of clothing you have **torn**?

_____

2. What time do you usually **awake** on weekdays?

_____

3. What do you like to **spread** on your bread?

_____

4. What did you do after you **left** school today?

_____

5. What would you like to **become** when you grow up?

_____

6. Have you ever been **bitten** by an insect? How did it feel?

_____

7. What did you **bring** to school in your backpack or bag today?

_____

8. Did you ever **find** something valuable? Tell what it was and how you found it.

_____

⭐ **Write a Character Sketch** Create a character who's about your age and who lived 500 years ago. Think about what the character looked like, what the character's favorite activities might have been, and what the character's chores might have been. Try to use at least three vocabulary words and three new verbs in your description.

Put Words Into Action

awake/awoke/awoken	find/found/found	spread/spread/spread
become/became/become	grind/ground/ground	spring/sprang/sprung
bite/bit/bitten	leave/left/left	swing/swung/swung
bring/brought/brought	rise/rose/risen	tear/tore/torn
creep/crept/crept	shed/shed/shed	understand/understood/ understood

Directions Each of the categories below contains a vocabulary word. In each box, list at least five things that fit in that category.

Things You Would Like to **Find**

1. _____
2. _____
3. _____
4. _____
5. _____

Things You Can **Spread**

6. _____
7. _____
8. _____
9. _____
10. _____

Things You Can **Swing**

11. _____
12. _____
13. _____
14. _____
15. _____

Things You Can **Tear**

16. _____
17. _____
18. _____
19. _____
20. _____

⭐ **Play the Word Game** Write the heading Things That _____ in your personal word journal. Choose one of your vocabulary words to fit the blank. (Do not choose a word used in the activity above.) Then challenge yourself to come up with at least five items that fit that category.

Review and Extend

awake/awoke/awoken
become/became/become
bite/bit/bitten
bring/brought/brought
creep/crept/crept

find/found/found
grind/ground/ground
leave/left/left
rise/rose/risen
shed/shed/shed

spread/spread/spread
spring/sprang/sprung
swing/swung/swung
tear/tore/torn
understand/understood/
understood

Learn More!

Irregular verbs don't follow the pattern of adding the ending *-d* or *–ed* to create the past tense or the past participle. The only way to learn these words is to memorize them.

Present Tense	Past Tense	Past Participle
awake	awoke	awoken
bring	brought	brought
shed	shed	shed

The past participle of a verb is the form you use after *has* or *have*.

The teacher *has left* the room. They *have torn* their tickets up.

Directions Choose the verb form that best fits the sentence. Write the word on the blank.

1. By the time the sun has _____ (*rise, rose, risen*), farmers are hard at work.

2. Farmers of long ago often _____ (*awake, awoke, awoken*) before dawn.

3. In earlier times, farmers _____ (*swing, swung*) long knives to cut down wheat.

4. Then, they _____ (*grind, ground*) the wheat to make flour.

5. A flour and water mixture called dough was baked and _____ (*become, became*) a loaf of bread.

 Go on a Word Hunt Find a set of directions or instructions in a textbook, magazine, or newspaper. You can also look for recipes or directions for how to build something. Identify four verbs that give you a clear picture of what to do. Write these verbs in your personal word journal. Also write the sentence in which you found the verb.

Check Your Mastery

Directions Choose the correct form of the verb and write it in the blank.

1. The tiger _____ (*spring, sprang, sprung*) out of the tall grass and

    chased the antelope.

2. A full moon has _____ (*rise, rose, risen*) high in the night sky.

3. Many mosquitoes have _____ (*bite, bit, bitten*) me this summer.

4. The alarm clock rang and Rita (*awake, awoke, awoken*) _____.

5. Doug was so angry that he _____ (*tear, tore, torn*) up the letter.

Directions Read each sentence. Then circle the correct verb to replace the words in boldface type.

6. The alligator **moved slowly and quietly** through the dark water.

    crept   **brought**   **left**

7. Bonnie **started to be** sad when she was told that she had to change classes.

    found   **became**   **awoke**

8. I **discovered** the keys that I lost yesterday.

    understood   **swung**   **found**

9. The cowboy **moved** the rope **back and forth** in the air and then roped the calf.

    swung   **spread**   **shed**

10. Dad **makes a powder of** coffee beans every morning for a fresh cup of coffee.

    brings   **tears**   **grinds**

Read Words in Context

An Art Show at School
by Sheena Ardell

"Let's put on the best art show this school has ever seen," said Mrs. Choi. "This class has so many **capable** students. You are all very talented and able to do great work. So I want you to put your talents to work."

Mrs. Choi's pep talk really inspired us. We worked for a month and set up the show. Everyone prepared carefully. No one was **sloppy**, or careless. We all wanted to do our best job.

Generous parents helped, too. They gave a lot of time and energy. They hung the works of art in the gym. They also made **tasty** cookies and other snacks.

Finally, the day of the show arrived. There were **numerous** paintings on display. An **enormous** oil painting by one of the students covered a whole wall of the gym. It was **immense**. The painting showed a **bitter** cold day in late December. Two people were out fishing on the lake.

On another wall were two smaller, **colorful** drawings. The swirls of bright color showed people dancing. A watercolor showed a **partial** view of a city street from an apartment window. You could see only the heads of the people down below. Another painting I liked was made up of **countless** dots of color. When you stood back from it, the many dots took the shape of a ship.

Some students painted plates and bowls. Each one had a clear and **distinct** pattern. Last but not least, Mrs. Choi presented a **bronze** sculpture she made showing a horse running.

The art show was declared an **absolute,** or complete, success. Such a **memorable** event will surely be talked about for years.

Connect Words and Meanings

absolute	capable	distinct	immense	partial
bitter	colorful	enormous	memorable	sloppy
bronze	countless	generous	numerous	tasty

Directions Look at the definitions on the left. Then circle the letter of the word on the right that best fits the definition. You may use the glossary to help you.

1. not complete   **A.** countless   **B.** partial   **C.** sloppy

2. very large   **A.** memorable   **B.** distinct   **C.** immense

3. give or share a lot   **A.** generous   **B.** capable   **C.** memorable

4. too many to count   **A.** sloppy   **B.** countless   **C.** distinct

5. complete, total   **A.** immense   **B.** distinct   **C.** absolute

6. worth remembering   **A.** memorable   **B.** bitter   **C.** immense

7. able to do something well   **A.** capable   **B.** generous   **C.** bronze

8. more than a few things   **A.** enormous   **B.** numerous   **C.** generous

9. upset and angry about something; very cold   **A.** partial   **B.** countless   **C.** bitter

10. made from a hard, brownish-gold metal; a reddish-brown color   **A.** colorful   **B.** sloppy   **C.** bronze

(continued on next page)

5 Adjectives to Know

Connect More Words and Meanings

absolute	capable	distinct	immense	partial
bitter	colorful	enormous	memorable	sloppy
bronze	countless	generous	numerous	tasty

Directions Match the vocabulary word on the left with the best synonym on the right. A synonym is a word that means the same thing. Write the letter in the blank. You may use the glossary to help you.

11. _____ distinct   **A.** delicious

12. _____ sloppy   **B.** huge

13. _____ enormous   **C.** one of a kind

14. _____ tasty   **D.** messy

15. _____ colorful   **E.** green or yellow, for example

Directions Use your knowledge of word meanings to choose the two vocabulary words that match each item below. Write them in the blank.

16. You might use these words to describe the size of an elephant. _____

17. You might use these words to describe the taste of something you eat. _____

18. You might use these words to describe the colors in a statue. _____

19. You might use these words to describe how many stars there are

   in the sky. _____

20. You might use these words to compare a king with complete power and one with

   only some power. _____

· ·

⭐ **Create a Word Web** Write the word *Art* in the center circle of a word web. Then write adjectives you could use to describe works of art (such as *interesting*) around the center circle. Write at least five new adjectives.

Use Words in Context

absolute	capable	distinct	immense	partial
bitter	colorful	enormous	memorable	sloppy
bronze	countless	generous	numerous	tasty

Directions Respond to each question below with a sentence that shows you understand the meaning of the word in boldface type. Write the sentence on the line.

1. What could a **generous** person give to someone else?

_____

2. What foods do you find to be most **tasty**?

_____

3. Why would someone want a **bronze** medal?

_____

4. How could you become a more **capable** student?

_____

5. What is something that is truly **countless**?

_____

6. What would a **sloppy** dresser wear?

_____

7. What experience might make a person feel **bitter**?

_____

8. Where would you be likely to find **enormous** animals?

_____

⭐ **Write an Ad** Work with a partner to write the copy words for an advertisement. Use new adjectives and the words *absolute*, *colorful*, *distinct*, *immense*, and *memorable*. Your ad could describe an event like a circus, a video, a movie, or something similar.

5 Adjectives to Know

Put Words Into Action

absolute	capable	distinct	immense	partial
bitter	colorful	enormous	memorable	sloppy
bronze	countless	generous	numerous	tasty

Directions Pretend to be talking to a word as if it were a person. Below are some interview questions to ask the word. Write the answers you think the word would give on the lines.

Questions to ask *ABSOLUTE*

1. What other words mean the same as you do?

   _____

   _____

2. What are you good at describing?

   _____

   _____

3. What don't you like? Why?

   _____

   _____

4. What advice would you give to students?

   _____

   _____

Questions to ask *IMMENSE*

5. What other words mean the same as you do?

   _____

   _____

6. What are you good at describing?

   _____

   _____

7. What don't you like? Why?

   _____

   _____

8. What advice would you give to kids?

   _____

   _____

⭐ **Be a Word** Working with a partner, take the role of a vocabulary word (other than *absolute* or *immense*) and answer your partner's questions. Your partner may ask the questions used above or create some new questions. Use your imagination and have fun being a "word." Write the questions and answers in your journal.

Review and Extend

absolute	capable	distinct	immense	partial
bitter	colorful	enormous	memorable	sloppy
bronze	countless	generous	numerous	tasty

Learn More! A word's **ending** may be a clue to the meaning and show that it is an adjective. Adjective endings can be:

–ful	–less	–y	–able	–ous
(means *full of*)	(means *without*)	(means *like* or *tending to*)	(means *able* or *can*)	(means *full of* or *having*)
colorful	countless	sloppy tasty	capable memorable	enormous generous numerous

Directions Write the correct vocabulary word in the blank space in each sentence. The words in boldface will give you a clue to the correct word. Then circle the adjective ending in each word.

1. Everyone will **remember** the author coming to school and reading from her novel.

It was a(n) _____ experience.

2. After she read, **many** students wanted her autograph. _____

students stood in line, waiting for her to sign her book.

3. The **huge** auditorium is large enough to hold a(n) _____ crowd.

It was **immense**.

4. He chose a **lively, bright green** paint to give the room a(n) _____

look.

5. The _____ writer **gave** the school **a thousand dollars**

to buy books for the library.

⭐ **Illustrate Words** Choose one of your vocabulary words. Draw a picture that illustrates this word. For example, to illustrate the word *sloppy*, you might draw a room with clothing thrown on the floor and the bed not made up. Write a sentence under the picture to describe it. Use your vocabulary word in your sentence.

5 Adjectives to Know

Check Your Mastery

Directions Circle the letter of the correct answer to each question.

1. Which of these might make things look more **distinct**?

   A. a picture   **B.** eyeglasses   **C.** a clock

2. Which of these is most likely to be an **immense** space?

   A. a bedroom   **B.** a closet   **C.** a sports stadium

3. How does a **bitter** person feel?

   A. angry   **B.** calm   **C.** joyful

4. What is an **absolute** mess like?

   A. completely messy   **B.** a little messy   **C.** not at all messy

5. What usually happens to a **capable** worker?

   A. gets a raise   **B.** is ignored   **C.** gets fired

Directions Read the sentences and the words that follow them. Then fill in the blank with the word choice that best fits the context.

6. The dancers wore _____ (*bronze, bitter, colorful*) costumes. They were red, yellow, blue, and purple.

7. Julio's birthday party was a _____ (*tasty, partial, memorable*) event. I'll never forget the fun we had.

8. Mr. Murphy is a _____ (*generous, numerous, sloppy*) man. He gives his time to many community projects.

9. Elisa gave a(n) _____ (*partial, enormous, capable*) answer to the question. She left out some important information.

10. Scientists say there are _____ (*countless, absolute, memorable*) stars in the sky. We may never know just how many there are.

Read Words in Context

READ!

Look Up–It's Time to Climb!

When I think about rock climbing, danger springs to mind. I imagine huge, **craggy** rocks or sharp, steep cliffs. Climbing a cliff is too **extreme** for me! I like sports that are a little more ordinary—at least that's what I thought until last Saturday!

Laurel and I were feeling **restless** just sitting around, so she talked me into climbing a rock! It was actually a rock wall at Barney's Gym. We signed up for a beginner's class. Luck was with us. We were **fortunate** that we got in because it was the most popular class.

The instructor, Aaron, told us that the wall has holes, or knobs, where you place your hands and feet to climb. Climbing holes come in many colors, so people create different routes using the colors. At first, Laurel and I were **bewildered** and a little confused. Aaron assured us that we'd learn quickly. He'd always be **available** to answer questions and help. I was a little **suspicious**. But then I decided to trust him.

It's **necessary** to wear a safety harness when you climb a wall. I felt **clumsy** and awkward at first. I thought I would never be able to do it. But I'm **stubborn.** I don't give up easily. It really makes me **furious** and angry with myself when I give up. Finally I got more comfortable. And it was worth it.

Reaching the top was an **incredible**, amazing experience.

That day, I decided to become a **permanent** member of the gym! I'll never be a professional, but being an **amateur** climber can be fun. There's a contest coming up soon! Laurel and I are reading about **modern**, up-to-date climbing equipment and skills. Maybe we'll have a chance to win.

Vocabulary Words

amateur	incredible
available	modern
bewildered	necessary
clumsy	permanent
craggy	restless
extreme	stubborn
fortunate	suspicious
furious	

Word Learning Tip!

Adjectives are words that describe a noun or pronoun. Adjectives can come before the noun or pronoun they are describing or after a linking verb. Linking verbs are verbs such as *is*, *are*, *was*, and *were*.

Vocabulary Building Strategy

Use Context Clues You can find the meaning of adjectives you don't know by using context clues. Think about the meanings of words around an unknown word. This will help you understand the meaning of an adjective you don't know.

6 More Adjectives to Know

Connect Words and Meanings

amateur	clumsy	fortunate	modern	restless
available	craggy	furious	necessary	stubborn
bewildered	extreme	incredible	permanent	suspicious

Directions Read each definition below. Circle the letter of the word that matches each definition. You may use the glossary to help you.

1. not professional; having to do with someone who takes part in a sport or activity for fun rather than for money

    A. stubborn   **B.** fortunate   **C.** amateur

2. not able to keep still or to concentrate

    A. suspicious   **B.** restless   **C.** clumsy

3. unbelievable or amazing

    A. incredible   **B.** craggy   **C.** available

4. confused or puzzled

    A. restless   **B.** bewildered   **C.** furious

5. lasting or meant to last for a long time; not expected to change

    A. permanent   **B.** incredible   **C.** modern

6. awkward and careless

    A. clumsy   **B.** amateur   **C.** bewildered

7. rugged and uneven

    A. necessary   **B.** craggy   **C.** furious

8. not busy; free to do things; ready to be used or bought

    A. incredible   **B.** permanent   **C.** available

9. up-to-date or new in style; having to do with the present

    A. modern   **B.** extreme   **C.** necessary

10. going beyond the ordinary or average; very great

    A. clumsy   **B.** modern   **C.** extreme

(continued on next page)

Connect More Words and Meanings

amateur	clumsy	fortunate	modern	restless
available	craggy	furious	necessary	stubborn
bewildered	extreme	incredible	permanent	suspicious

Directions Each item below has a vocabulary word followed by a group of three words. Two of the words in the group are synonyms for the vocabulary word. They have almost the same or a similar meaning. Circle the word that does not fit in the group. You may use your glossary or a dictionary to help you.

11. furious · · · · · · · · · · · **angry** · · · · **fierce** · · · · **calm**

12. necessary · · · · · · · · · **extra** · · · · **needed** · · · · **important**

13. stubborn · · · · · · · · · · **willful** · · · · **determined** · · · · **tame**

14. fortunate · · · · · · · · · **lucky** · · · · **favorable** · · · · **unlucky**

15. suspicious · · · · · · · · **sure** · · · · **distrustful** · · · · **doubting**

16. available · · · · · · · · · · **free** · · · · **busy** · · · · **open**

17. restless · · · · · · · · · · · **peaceful** · · · · **nervous** · · · · **uneasy**

18. bewildered · · · · · · · · **confused** · · · · **certain** · · · · **puzzled**

19. craggy · · · · · · · · · · · · **smooth** · · · · **rough** · · · · **jagged**

20. extreme · · · · · · · · · · **average** · · · · **greatest** · · · · **highest**

Name That Sport Work with a partner and brainstorm different sports or activities that you might like to try but never have. Select a vocabulary word to go with each sport that describes your doing that sport. For example, you might be a "furious ice skater" because you get angry at yourself for falling down. Or you might be a "permanent baseball player" because you love this sport. Challenge yourself to use all 15 adjectives.

6 More Adjectives to Know

Use Words in Context

amateur	clumsy	fortunate	modern	restless
available	craggy	furious	necessary	stubborn
bewildered	extreme	incredible	permanent	suspicious

Directions Complete each sentence below. Write your answer on the blank line. Make sure your sentence fits the meaning of the boldface word.

1. The girl felt **bewildered** when she _____

_____ .

2. Because Renee doesn't want to stay an **amateur** piano player, she _____

_____ .

3. The mountain was so **craggy** that _____

_____ .

4. Shane was so **stubborn** that _____

_____ .

5. Because we were feeling **restless**, we _____

_____ .

6. Janeen feels **clumsy** when she tries to _____

_____ .

7. Cooking on a **modern** stove is easier than cooking on an old-fashioned one because _____

_____ .

8. The most **incredible** sight I ever saw was _____

_____ .

⭐ **Make Word Cards** Choose three vocabulary words. Write each word on the front of an index card. Draw a picture illustrating the word on the back of the card. For example, for the word *restless*, you could draw a tiger pacing back and forth in his cage. Write a sentence using the word under each picture.

Put Words Into Action

amateur	clumsy	**fortunate**	modern	restless
available	craggy	**furious**	necessary	stubborn
bewildered	extreme	**incredible**	permanent	suspicious

Directions Create a word map for the word *fortunate*. Provide two synonyms and antonyms for the word. Give two examples of things the word could describe, and give two non-examples, too. A non-example shows something the word doesn't describe at all.

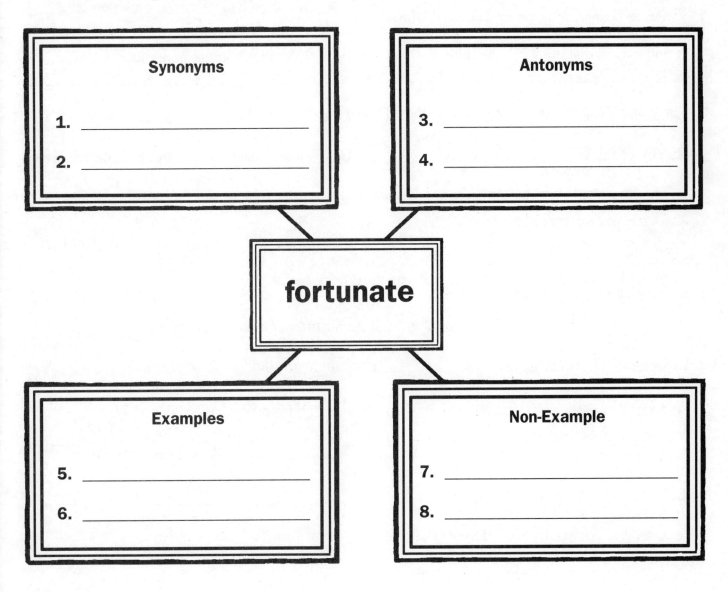

Synonyms

1. _____

2. _____

Antonyms

3. _____

4. _____

fortunate

Examples

5. _____

6. _____

Non-Example

7. _____

8. _____

★ **Create Word Maps** Choose three other vocabulary words. Create word maps for these words.

6 More Adjectives to Know

Review and Extend

amateur	clumsy	fortunate	modern	restless
available	craggy	furious	necessary	stubborn
bewildered	extreme	incredible	permanent	suspicious

Learn More! **Adjectives** often come after **linking verbs.** Some linking verbs are: *be, feel, look, seem, appear, become, taste, sound,* and *stay.* A linking verb is a link between the subject of a sentence and a word that describes the subject.

The chocolate cake tastes delicious.

The baseball game was memorable.

That mountain looks enormous.

The song sounds beautiful.

Directions Read each sentence. Choose the adjective that best fits. Write the word in the blank.

1. The coach is _____ (*suspicious, extreme, fortunate*) of the referees.

He does not think they are treating his team fairly.

2. It is _____ (*permanent, craggy, necessary*) to wear light,

spiked shoes to climb a wall so that you can move easily.

3. There were no tickets left for the Big Rock Adventure. Then one ticket became

_____ (*incredible, available, extreme*).

4. Some climbers create amazing routes up the wall. These routes are

_____(*restless, suspicious, incredible*).

5. Indoor climbing is a fast-growing and very _____

(*modern, clumsy, available*) sport that can be a lot of fun.

Give a Pep Talk Imagine that your school soccer team is losing by 2 points with about 10 minutes left to play. Write a pep talk that the coach might give. What descriptive adjectives might the coach use to inspire the team to try a little harder? Use four vocabulary words and four new adjectives.

Check Your Mastery

Directions Complete each sentence below. Make sure your sentence fits the meaning of the boldface word.

1. If a table at a restaurant is **available**, it is _____.

2. If someone is **clumsy**, he might _____.

3. If a person is **stubborn**, she would _____.

4. If a detective felt **suspicious**, he would _____.

5. If an athlete is an **amateur**, she would not _____.

Directions Choose the word that fits best in the blank in each sentence. Circle the letter of the word you choose.

6. Juan was _____ to learn how to play baseball from his father.
   A. extreme   **B.** bewildered   **C.** fortunate   **D.** modern

7. The gymnasts were puzzled by the other team's actions and felt _____.
   A. bewildered   **B.** incredible   **C.** necessary   **D.** permanent

8. Everything in our new gym is _____ and up-to-date.
   A. restless   **B.** modern   **C.** craggy   **D.** furious

9. Sean played an amazing game today! His team was losing by 1 point with 30 seconds left when Sean made a(n) _____ basket to score 2 points.
   A. clumsy   **B.** permanent   **C.** amateur   **D.** incredible

10. The basketball coach was hired for only one season. However, when her team won the championship, her job became _____.
   A. clumsy   **B.** permanent   **C.** amateur   **D.** incredible

Read Words in Context

Vocabulary Words

accidentally	merely
almost	occasionally
certainly	onward
comfortably	powerfully
downright	recently
especially	steadily
gradually	usually
instead	

Word Learning Tip!

Adverbs are words that describe verbs, adjectives, or other adverbs. Many adverbs end in *–ly*, but some do not. Adverbs can come before or after the word they describe and tell *how, when,* or *where* an action happens.

Vocabulary Building Strategy

Use Context Clues You can find the meaning of adverbs you don't know by studying their context. Put together the meanings of the words around an unknown adverb. This will help you understand the unfamiliar word's meaning.

READ!

Betsy Ross and the American Flag

Betsy Ross made the first flag for the new American nation. Mrs. Ross was a seamstress in Philadelphia. Her husband had been killed **accidentally** in January of 1776. He died in an explosion that no one had predicted. So **recently**, or not long ago, Mrs. Ross had become a widow.

Betsy Ross had to work to support her family. This was difficult, and she had **almost** given up hope of getting work when she received a visit from George Washington. General Washington had decided that creating a new flag was **especially** important to boost the spirit of his army. He asked Betsy to make it, and she told him that she would gladly take the job.

A loyal patriot, Mrs. Ross felt **downright** proud to be fashioning the first flag for the new country. She suggested that it have 13 stars to represent the 13 new states. She did not want to use 5-pointed stars. She recommended using 6-pointed ones **instead**.

General Washington and Mrs. Ross worked **comfortably** together. He agreed with most of her suggestions. Together they **gradually** came up with a perfect design. The new flag had 7 white stripes and 6 red ones. The stripes stood for the 13 colonies. In the left-hand corner was a circle of 13 stars on blue cloth.

Betsy Ross began sewing and worked **steadily** for a month. **Occasionally,** she worried that her flag would not be accepted, but she **certainly** had no need to fear. The new flag affected Washington's soldiers **powerfully**. A country's flag **usually** makes people feel proud. But this was not **merely** a flag; it was a symbol of hope. It helped the soldiers march **onward** through difficult times.

Connect Words and Meanings

accidentally	comfortably	gradually	occasionally	recently
almost	downright	instead	onward	steadily
certainly	especially	merely	powerfully	usually

Directions Read each definition below. Then read the sentence that follows the definition. Choose the vocabulary word from the list that matches the definition and fits in the sentence. Write it in the blank. You may use the glossary to help you.

1. from time to time

Most of the time, I like to read books about today. _____,
I enjoy reading historical fiction.

2. completely, totally

We laughed and laughed at the dog's antics. They were _____ silly.

3. slowly, bit by bit

You can't stop change. It happens _____ over time.

4. forward

The mountains were difficult to pass, but the pioneers pressed _____ .

5. surely, definitely

Keisha is my best friend. _____, she will come to my party.

6. in a very strong way

The general spoke _____ to the soldiers. He told them to have courage.

7. very nearly

It's been _____ a year since I started taking swimming lessons.

8. more than is common; particularly

Kari's parents were _____ proud when she won the soccer medal.

(continued on next page)

Connect More Words and Meanings

accidentally	comfortably	gradually	occasionally	recently
almost	downright	instead	onward	steadily
certainly	especially	merely	powerfully	usually

Directions Continue connecting words and meanings. Read each definition below. Then read the sentence that follows the definition. Choose the vocabulary word from the list that matches the definition and fits in the sentence. Write it in the blank. You may use the glossary to help you.

9. continuously, without stopping

The wind blew _____ throughout the night.

10. just, only, simply

It was _____ a scratch, not a serious wound.

11. in a relaxed way

Marta sat _____ on the soft, cushy sofa.

12. in place of another

Levar didn't want to play baseball. He wanted to play soccer _____ .

13. a short time ago

Frankie could tell every detail of the movie. She had seen it _____ .

14. most of the time; normally

_____ , Lee goes on his own to camp in the summer.

This year, he is taking a trip with his parents.

15. in a way that is unexpected

The playful kitten _____ knocked the glass vase off the table.

· ·

⭐ **Draw the Flag** Draw the current flag of the United States. Write a few sentences under the flag telling about it. Use at least three adverbs in your sentences. Two adverbs should be from the vocabulary list.

Use Words in Context

accidentally	comfortably	gradually	occasionally	recently
almost	downright	instead	onward	steadily
certainly	especially	merely	powerfully	usually

Directions Write a vocabulary word in the blank in each item. Use the context clues in boldface to help you choose the best word.

1. _____ , I am learning to speak Spanish. **Little by little**, I learn new words and phrases.
(*Steadily, Instead, Gradually*)

2. I will sleep _____ under such a **soft, warm blanket**.
(*comfortably, downright, recently*)

3. If I won a **really big prize**, I would feel _____ happy. I would be **very** glad.
(*downright, steadily, usually*)

4. Did you receive the letter _____ or have you **had it for quite a while**?
(*almost, occasionally, recently*)

5. Most people would be _____ motivated by **a reward of a thousand dollars**. They would want to help **more than** they usually would.
(*especially, onward, merely*)

6. If it rains **all day**, it is raining _____ .
(*instead, comfortably, steadily*)

7. If you **didn't mean to** spill the juice, then it happened _____ .
(*powerfully, accidentally, certainly*)

8. When the parade moves **forward**, it goes _____ .
(*onward, almost, usually*)

9. **Once in a while**, Yasmin writes a poem. She writes _____ , but **not often**.
(*accidentally, occasionally, powerfully*)

10. Paco hit the ball so _____ that it **went out of the ballpark**.
(*occasionally, powerfully, merely*)

Write in Your Journal Write about the things you do to get ready for school in the morning. Use at least three vocabulary words to describe your morning routine.

Put Words Into Action

accidentally	comfortably	gradually	occasionally	recently
almost	downright	instead	onward	steadily
certainly	especially	merely	powerfully	usually

Directions Sort the adverbs in the vocabulary list according to what they tell about verbs and other words. Write the adverbs on the lines.

Adverbs That Tell How

1. I was sleeping _____ .
2. The glass broke _____ .
3. Rita learned to speak Spanish _____ over time.

Adverbs That Tell When

4. The snow was still on the ground. It snowed _____ .

Adverbs That Tell Where

5. We wouldn't give up. We kept moving _____ .

Adverbs That Tell How Often

6. Jason practiced not every day but only _____ .
7. His sister practiced _____ every day.

Adverbs That Tell How Much

8. Vicky was _____ certain she would get on the team.
9. His behavior after the game was _____ foolish.
10. I was _____ pleased to receive the gift.

 Find Additional Adverbs Brainstorm with a partner. Try to come up with at least one additional adverb to fit in each box. Write it in the box next to the heading.

Review and Extend

accidentally	comfortably	gradually	occasionally	recently
almost	downright	instead	onward	steadily
certainly	especially	merely	powerfully	usually

Learn More! An **adverb** tells more about a verb, an adjective, or another adverb. An **adjective** tells more about a noun or a pronoun. Often, you can form an adverb by adding –ly to an adjective.

Adjective		Adverb
mere	+ –ly	merely
gradual	+ –ly	gradually

Directions Read each sentence below. Notice the adjective in boldface. Add –ly to the adjective to form the adverb. Write the adverb in the blank. Then write your own sentence using this adverb.

1. She was **certain** her design would work. It was _____ a good design.

2. Sentence: _____

3. It is **usual** that a flag is wider than it is long. Flags are _____ wider than long.

4. Sentence: _____

5. Her life was quite **comfortable**. She lived _____ on her earnings from sewing.

6. Sentence: _____

7. His choice was not **accidental**. He did not choose her _____.

8. Sentence: _____

9. She had an **occasional** job. She worked _____.

10. Sentence: _____

★ **Create an Adjective-to-Adverb Chart** Search through textbooks, magazines, and newspapers to find four adverbs that were formed by adding –ly to an adjective. Create a chart showing how each adverb was formed. Use the chart at the top of this page as your model.

Check Your Mastery

Directions Choose the word in parentheses that best fits in the blank. Write it in the blank.

1. Flag Day is celebrated on June 14. It has been celebrated on that day from 1877

_____ (*onward, recently, accidentally*).

2. Flag Day is an _____ (*almost, instead, especially*) popular

holiday with Americans who want to show their patriotism.

3. Some Americans _____ (*usually, gradually, accidentally*) fly their flags

on June 14 as well as on Memorial Day and Independence Day.

4. _____ (*Merely, Almost, Instead*) all public schools have a special

Flag Day celebration.

5. Some towns and cities are so _____ (*downright, comfortably, onward*)

proud of the flag that they hold a special parade.

6. Flag Day _____ (*especially, recently, gradually*) became accepted

as a holiday. It took from 1877 to 1916 to become widely celebrated.

7. It was a tireless schoolteacher who worked _____

(*steadily, downright, almost*) over the years to make Flag Day a holiday in every state.

8. The American flag is a strong symbol of American identity. It _____

(*powerfully, merely, occasionally*) represents the national spirit.

9. The Great Star flag of 1818 was _____ (*certainly, occasionally, gradually*)

different from earlier flags. It had twenty stars, arranged in a star shape.

10. Hawaii is the state that most _____ (*powerfully, recently, steadily*)

joined the United States. It became a state in 1959.

Read Words in Context

READ!

What's the Scoop?

Johari, Neal, and their friends decided to start a weekly newspaper. "The first thing we must decide is how much we can **charge** for each issue," said Neal. They agreed that 25 cents was neither too little nor too much. "So a **quarter** is a fair price," Neal stated.

"Okay," Johari said, "let's talk about features." Luke suggested Sports Scoops, stories about sports events. Justin had an idea for a feature called Photo of the Week, but then changed his title to Click Picks. Everyone liked that name much better than his **initial** idea. Ayana suggested Science Sneaks— stories about **rare** and unusual animals in nature.

After about a one-hour **period** of discussion, Neal said in a **firm** manner, "Let's get down to business. We have to decide the **content** of the articles for the **current** issue. What should the articles in our first issue be about?"

Johari added, "Let's be **patient** and listen to everyone's ideas. You never know how one not-so-great idea can lead to a fantastic one. Look at the number of newspapers sold in **relation** to the number of interesting articles. More good articles mean more people buy the newspaper. It's our **sole** and only goal to create a really interesting newspaper. But it wouldn't be bad to make some money, too."

Ayana suggested an article about Jennifer Clark, the newscaster for **Channel** 25—a local TV station. Ayana said that she'd call to see if the station manager would **permit** two of them to interview her. Then Eduardo suggested an article about the Hayloft Restaurant, which was in an old horse **stable.** "It's really cool," he said. "Customers sit on huge bales of hay up in the hayloft! They also have the best **mint** ice cream in the city!"

"Ice cream!" responded Lily. "Now you're talking. I vote that we go to the Hayloft right now and finish our plans there!"

Vocabulary Words

channel	period
charge	permit
content	quarter
current	rare
firm	relation
initial	sole
mint	stable
patient	

Word Learning Tip!

A **multiple-meaning word** has two or more very different meanings. The meaning of the word depends on how the word is being used in the sentence. A multiple-meaning word might be used as a noun, a verb, or an adjective. Understanding the part of speech of the word in a sentence will help you determine its meaning.

Vocabulary Building Strategy

Use Context Clues Context clues help you identify the meaning of a multiple-meaning word. Use context clues to choose the meaning that makes sense in the sentence that the word is in.

Connect Words and Meanings

channel	current	mint	permit	relation
charge	firm	patient	quarter	sole
content	initial	period	rare	stable

Directions Read each sentence. Then read the two definitions for the boldface word. Circle the letter of the definition that best matches how the boldface word is used.

1. Gregory wrote a great story about a whale that swam up the **channel** and got lost.
   A. a TV or radio station
   B. a narrow stretch of water between two pieces of land

2. Sammy decided to take **charge** of the meeting because everyone was talking at the same time.
   A. to ask someone to pay a certain price
   B. control or command of something

3. Rosa was **content** to write poems every week for the newspaper.
   A. happy and satisfied
   B. the information in a piece of writing; what makes it up

4. Here's the most **current** information we have about solar storms.
   A. movement of water in a river or ocean, or if electricity, in a wire
   B. happening now, up-to-date

5. Her voice was gentle, but **firm,** when she told the reporter to check the facts of his article.
   A. confident and strong
   B. a business or company

6. Tracy's **initial** reaction was disbelief. She couldn't believe Donna had written the story.
   A. first or at the beginning
   B. the first letter of a name or word

7. Martina forgot to put a **period** at the end of the sentence.
   A. the punctuation mark that ends a sentence
   B. a length of time

8. Jessica wrote an article about a rabbit that likes **mint** leaves better than carrots.
   A. a plant whose leaves have a strong, pleasant smell
   B. a place where coins and bills are made

(continued on next page)

Connect More Words and Meanings

channel	current	mint	permit	relation
charge	firm	patient	quarter	sole
content	initial	period	rare	stable

Directions Continue the activity. Read each sentence. Then read the two definitions for the bold-face word. Circle the letter of the definition that best matches how the boldface word is used.

9. Mrs. Ramirez worked at the hospital when Jaime was a **patient** there.
   A. a person treated by a doctor or other health worker
   B. able to wait calmly for a result, not hasty

10. Latoya's older brother just received his driver's **permit**.
   A. a document giving someone the right to do something
   B. to allow something

11. The town voted to **quarter** the troops in the library.
   A. one of four parts or a coin representing one fourth of a dollar
   B. to house or furnish with housing

12. Reese liked to eat his steak **rare**.
   A. not often found, seen, or occurring
   B. cooked very lightly

13. My cousin Alexis is my favorite **relation**.
   A. a member of one's family
   B. a connection between two or more things

14. I bet you will laugh if I tickle the **sole** of your foot with a feather.
   A. only or single
   B. bottom part of a foot, shoe, or boot

15. The house can withstand a hurricane; it is quite **stable**.
   A. a building where houses or cows are kept
   B. solid and steady

BONUS Write a sentence that includes three of the vocabulary words.

⭐ **Write Headlines** Imagine you are working on a newspaper. Your job is to write headlines for two news stories. The trick is that in each headline, you should use the same vocabulary word. But you must use one meaning of the word in the first headline and another meaning of that same word in the second headline. For example: *The Sole Survivor of the Claremount Disaster Tells Her Story* and *Are You Being Overcharged? Why Getting a Sole on Your Shoe Can Cost an Arm and a Leg.*

Use Words in Context

channel	current	mint	permit	relation
charge	firm	patient	quarter	sole
content	initial	period	rare	stable

Directions Read each group of sentences below. Circle the letter of the sentence in which the boldface word has the same meaning as in the numbered sentence.

1. Our class's **current** project is running a refreshment stand to raise money for stray animals.
  A. The **current** in that river is very strong and often changes direction.
  B. The **current** news is that our class project has raised about $100.

2. We sell brownies at the stand and **charge** 50 cents apiece for them.
  A. Some people **charge** a lot more for brownies.
  B. Lucy is the person in **charge** of the refreshment stand.

3. For every dollar we make, we donate a **quarter** to the animal shelter.
  A. Do you think we can **quarter** the soldiers in the factory?
  B. Our cookies cost a **quarter** each.

4. Our parents **permit** us to make the cookies and brownies at home.
  A. My mom and dad **permit** us to use the kitchen on Saturday mornings.
  B. We don't need a **permit** for the refreshment stand.

5. Our brownies are so good that the TV cooking **channel** wants to interview us.
  A. The sightseeing boat on the **channel** buys our brownies for their snack bar.
  B. Flip the dial to another radio **channel**.

6. Our **initial** batch of brownies was delicious because we added extra chocolate.
  A. The **initial** comments about the stand were very good.
  B. I write my **initial** on each brownie wrapper along with the date.

7. Everyone was **firm** in the decision to make ginger cookies for the stand.
  A. The law **firm** where Jonathan's father works printed the flyers for us.
  B. We were **firm** about the art we wanted for our refreshment stand flyers.

8. The carpenter took a long time to build the stand, but we tried to be **patient**.
  A. Cooks must be **patient**, or they will make mistakes.
  B. The **patient** in the hospital received gifts of food and flowers.

⭐ **Start a Company** Work in small groups and brainstorm ideas about companies that would be fun to start. Choose one company and write about what you have to do to get the business going by a certain date. Try to include at least three vocabulary words and two new multiple-meaning words in your time line.

Put Words Into Action

channel	current	mint	permit	relation
charge	firm	patient	quarter	sole
content	initial	period	rare	stable

Directions Read each clue. Then write the vocabulary word that describes the clue.

1. Clue: You might order an ice cream made with this flavor.

chocolate _____

2. Clue: You might want a piece of jewelry with this on it.

your _____

3. Clue: You might use this to play a game at an amusement park.

a _____

4. Clue: Your sister, uncle, cousin, or aunt is this person.

your _____

5. Clue: You might go to this place to ride horses.

a _____

6. Clue: When you ask a question, you use a question mark instead of this.

a _____

7. Clue: If you found a gem like this, it could be worth a lot of money.

a _____ gem

8. Clue: If you are very happy because you did a good deed, you might feel like this.

_____

9. Clue: You might use a remote control to change this.

a _____

10. Clue: If you don't pay for something with cash, you might do this.

_____ it

· ·

⭐ **Write Puns and Riddles** Puns and riddles are types of wordplay that may use the multiple meanings of a word for fun. Write a pun or riddle that uses the same word in two different ways. For example: *What do you call someone who has waited too long in a doctor's office? A no-longer patient patient.*

Multiple-Meaning Words to Know

Review and Extend

channel	current	mint	permit	relation
charge	firm	patient	quarter	sole
content	initial	period	rare	stable

Learn More! Multiple-meaning words may have different meanings when they are used as different parts of speech in sentences. Some multiple-meaning words can be nouns and verbs. Others can be nouns and adjectives. Here are some examples:

Noun	Verb	Noun	Adjective
permit	to permit	a sole	sole
a fishing permit	permit him to go	the sole of your shoe	the sole reason

Directions Read each pair of sentences. Look at how the boldface word is used. Circle the correct part of speech for each boldface word.

1. Louisa gave Sam a **quarter** to buy a grape juice.   verb   noun

2. She told him to please return in a **quarter** of an hour for the meeting.   verb   noun

3. Pam's **initial** idea was to have the newspaper staff meet weekly.   verb   adjective

4. She was happy to **initial** the memo she received from the editor.   verb   adjective

5. Lucia thought an article about saving the old horse **stable** was great.   adjective   noun

6. The horses needed a safe, **stable** place to live.   adjective   noun

7. Billy and Samantha got a **permit** to hand out free newspapers on the corner.   verb   noun

8. The town will **permit** them to give the papers away from 9 A.M. to 6 P.M.   verb   noun

9. Josie worked very hard on the **content** of the article.   adjective   noun

10. She felt **content** with the report when she handed it to the editor.   adjective   noun

⭐ **Word Jam/Poetry Slam!** Imagine that one of the features in your newspaper is Word Jam/Poetry Slam! Work with a partner and brainstorm ideas for poems. To get started, write a very short story in your journal. Now turn it into a poem. Then read the words out loud. Is there a beat? If you get stuck with the beat, keep trying. Reread the words out loud until you get a word rhythm. Try to use at least two vocabulary words and a new multiple-meaning word if possible.

Check Your Mastery

Directions Read each question. Circle the letter of the correct answer.

1. Which of the following can you get at a **mint**?

   A. coins   **B.** clothes   **C.** candies

2. Which one of these can travel on a **channel**?

   A. an airplane   **B.** a ferry boat   **C.** a horse

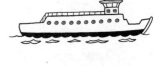

3. For which of these activities do you need a **permit**?

   A. learning to drive   **B.** riding a bike   **C.** writing a book

4. On which of the following would you find a **sole**?

   A. a shirt   **B.** a hat   **C.** a shoe

5. Which of these is a **rare** event?

   A. a rainstorm   **B.** a windstorm   **C.** an eclipse

Directions Read each sentence. Replace the boldface word(s) in each sentence with the vocabulary word that best fits. Circle this word.

6. Marianna enjoyed the **topic and information** in that story very much.

   charge   content   relation

7. The **time** in which we live is sometimes called "The Information Age."

   quarter   period   stable

8. The scientist discovered an **uncommon** type of frog living in the pond.

   initial   rare   mint

9. Who is on the cover of the **most recent** issue of that magazine?

   current   firm   permit

10. I didn't know that you are a **family member** of a famous news reporter.

   relation   patient   channel

Read Words in Context

The Accident

Josh's grandma **cautioned** him about going down the back stairs. She **warned** him not to use them until they were fixed. The stairs were **old**, but lots of things in Grandma's house were old. She called these things **antique**, meaning that, in addition to being old, they may have been valuable. The spinning wheel and the rocking chair, for example, were both made by hand a long time ago.

Josh meant to stay away from the back stairs. But one morning, he heard a loud noise in the backyard. Josh got very excited. That's when he made his **blunder**. He made the **mistake** of running down the back stairs because they were the closest to the yard. About halfway down, a stair split in two. Josh fell and began **hollering**. When he **shouted**, Grandma came running. At first, she began to yell at Josh because he hadn't minded her. Then she saw that he was really hurt. He was **clenching** his right ankle with his hand and moaning in pain. Grandma **clasped** Josh's hand with hers and said, "I'm calling the **doctor** right now."

Doctor Chen was Grandma's **physician**. "You seem to have **fractured** or perhaps broken your ankle, young man," he said. "We'll have to get an X ray to see if you **shattered** your bone into little pieces."

Josh had a **hunch** that he would be walking on crutches. His **guess** was correct. Yet, he found **creative** and **inventive** ways to get help when he needed it. He put together an electric buzzer so that he could call Grandma when he needed her. Grandma thought the invention was great, but Josh was **modest** about it. He didn't brag because the accident had made him feel pretty **humble**. He was not proud that he had disobeyed his grandmother and used the broken stairs.

Connect Words and Meanings

antique	clench	guess	inventive	physician
blunder	creative	holler	mistake	shatter
caution	doctor	humble	modest	shout
clasp	fracture	hunch	old	warn

Directions Read each numbered clue below. Then complete the crossword puzzle. You may use the glossary to help you.

ACROSS

2. to hold somebody or something with the hands or arms; a synonym for *clench*

6. a break, split, or crack in an object or a material; a synonym for *shatter*

8. to speak in a loud or angry voice; a synonym for *holler*

10. to call out or use a loud voice; a synonym for *shout*

12. a formal word for someone trained to treat sick people; a synonym for *doctor*

15. not new or not young; a synonym for *antique*

16. not having or expressing a high opinion of your own achievements or abilities; a synonym for *humble*

17. to tell someone something about a danger or bad thing that might happen; a synonym for *caution*

18. not new and probably valuable; a synonym for *old*

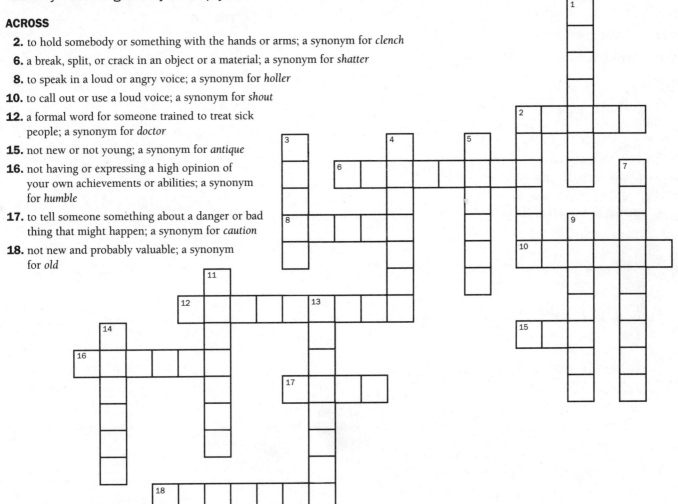

DOWN

1. an error or misunderstanding; a synonym for *blunder*

2. to hold or grip tightly or to close your teeth or fist tightly; a synonym for *clasp*

3. to form an opinion without knowing for sure; a synonym for *hunch*

4. to advise someone that something is risky or dangerous; a synonym for *warn*

5. unassuming in attitude and behavior; a synonym for *modest*

7. displaying creativity or imagination in its design; a synonym for *creative*

9. a foolish error; a synonym for *mistake*

11. to break or cause something to break suddenly into many small, brittle pieces; a synonym for *fracture*

13. using or showing use of the imagination to form new ideas or things; a synonym for *inventive*

14. a more casual way of referring to someone who treats sick people; a synonym for *physician*

Connect More Words and Meanings

antique	clench	guess	inventive	physician
blunder	creative	holler	mistake	shatter
caution	doctor	humble	modest	shout
clasp	fracture	hunch	old	warn

Directions Read each group of words below. Write the two words in each group that are synonyms.

Synonyms

1. creative, dull, inventive, blunder _____ _____

2. antique, gossip, caution, warn _____ _____

3. new, clasp, antique, old _____ _____

4. modest, shatter, fracture, repair _____ _____

5. clasp, drop, clench, shout _____ _____

6. modest, blunder, boastful, humble _____ _____

7. warn, physician, doctor, nurse _____ _____

8. blunder, correct, mistake, caution _____ _____

9. holler, shout, whisper, inventive _____ _____

10. hunch, guess, mistake, fact _____ _____

⭐ **Write About an Invention** Think about a modern invention, such as the cell phone, the VCR, or the DVD. Write a paragraph comparing and contrasting it with a device it replaced. Use the words *old, antique, inventive, warn, hunch, creative, guess, humble,* and *modest* in your paragraphs, and two new synonyms as well.

Use Words in Context

antique	clench	guess	inventive	physician
blunder	creative	holler	mistake	shatter
caution	doctor	humble	modest	shout
clasp	fracture	hunch	old	warn

Directions Answer the question by writing a sentence on the blank line. Use the boldface word in your sentence.

1. Why would an object be called **antique**?

_____

2. What **hunch** of yours turned out to be true?

_____

3. What is the most **creative** thing that you have ever done?

_____

4. Do you think it's better to be **humble** or proud?

_____

5. What can you learn from a **blunder** that you make?

_____

6. What would you **warn** a younger kid about?

_____

7. How could you **fracture** a bone?

_____

8. When is it always a good idea to **shout**?

_____

⭐ **Play Synonym Matchup** On a sheet of paper, draw a vertical line down the center of the page. Put all the words on the vocabulary list in synonym pairs, one synonym on each side of the line. Time how long it takes you to match each word with its synonym.

Put Words Into Action

antique	clench	guess	inventive	physician
blunder	creative	holler	mistake	shatter
caution	doctor	humble	modest	shout
clasp	fracture	hunch	old	warn

Directions Look at each picture. Read the definition. Then write the synonyms that match the definition. Finally, write a sentence using one of the synonyms to describe the picture.

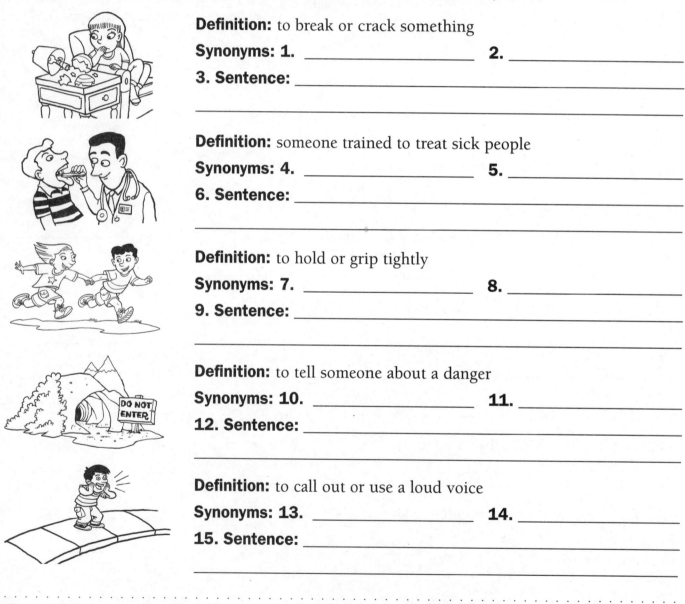

Definition: to break or crack something

Synonyms: **1.** _____ **2.** _____

3. Sentence: _____

_____

Definition: someone trained to treat sick people

Synonyms: **4.** _____ **5.** _____

6. Sentence: _____

_____

Definition: to hold or grip tightly

Synonyms: **7.** _____ **8.** _____

9. Sentence: _____

_____

Definition: to tell someone about a danger

Synonyms: **10.** _____ **11.** _____

12. Sentence: _____

_____

Definition: to call out or use a loud voice

Synonyms: **13.** _____ **14.** _____

15. Sentence: _____

_____

⭐ **Create a Synonym Pie** Draw a circle on a piece of paper. Divide it into five parts. Choose one of the synonym pairs and write each word in a sentence on one piece of the pie. Then find three other synonyms to write in sentences on the other slices. You can use a dictionary, thesaurus, or glossary to help you.

Review and Extend

antique	clench	guess	inventive	physician
blunder	creative	holler	mistake	shatter
caution	doctor	humble	modest	shout
clasp	fracture	hunch	old	warn

Learn More! Some synonyms have small differences in meaning. These small differences are called **shades of meaning**. One synonym may have a more positive meaning than another (*antique/*old) or one may be more formal than another (*instructor/*teacher).

Synonyms can also show degrees of intensity or strength. A *frigid* day is *colder* than a *cool* day. Although *frigid, cold,* and *cool* are all synonyms, there are shades of difference in their meanings.

Directions Answer the following questions about shades of meaning in the synonyms. Write your answer in a complete sentence in the blank.

1. Which do you think is more embarrassing—a **blunder** or a **mistake**?

Why? _____

2. Which word—**physician** or **doctor**—would you be more likely to use in a letter to a friend?

Why? _____

3. Would you rather someone **clasp** your hand or **clench** it?

Why? _____

4. Which of the synonyms—**shout** or **holler**—would you be less likely to use in a formal school

essay? Why? _____

5. Which word—**warn** or **caution**—would you put on a bottle of poison?

Why? _____

Write a Letter Write an informal letter to a friend in which you describe an accident that you or someone you know had. Use one synonym from at least two of the sets of synonyms in the vocabulary word list. Underline the synonyms you used. Be prepared to explain why you chose one synonym over the other.

Check Your Mastery

Directions Read each item below. Choose the word in parentheses that best fits the context. Write it on the line.

1. Thomas Edison invented the electric light and the phonograph. He was a very

_____(creative, humble, antique) person.

2. Do you think it is difficult to stay _____(modest, inventive,

fracture) when you are praised by presidents and heads of great corporations?

3. When he was twelve years old, Edison was hit in the head. Years later, he told a famous

_____(mistake, doctor, holler) that the blow

caused him to slowly lose his hearing.

4. Young Edison did experiments with chemicals in the baggage cars of trains. Once he made

the _____ (guess, blunder, shatter) of setting the train car on fire.

5. Edison once saw a railroad car heading straight for a boy. Edison quickly

_____(shattered, warned, hunch) the boy and saved his life.

6. When Edison was concentrating very hard on an experiment, he was sometimes seen to

_____(clench, caution, shout) his teeth in determination.

7. Edison had an inspired _____ (hunch, physician, clasp).

He believed he could record sound, and he proved it when he invented the phonograph.

8. Have you ever seen the _____(clasp, antique, yell)

record player that Edison invented in 1877?

9. As Edison grew older, he became more deaf. He had trouble hearing people even if they

_____(shouted, fractured, cautioned) right into his ear.

10. In 1879, Edison produced the first electric light. People were amazed that the heat from

the electricity did not _____(shatter, clench, blunder) the glass bulb.

Read Words in Context

READ!

The Great Detective

One of the most famous detectives in the world is not a real person but a fictional character. He is Sherlock Holmes, the main character in a series of stories by the British writer Sir Arthur Conan Doyle. In the stories, Sherlock Holmes solves mysteries with the help of his best friend, Dr. Watson.

Holmes can find clues to a crime where other people see nothing. What they barely **glimpse**, Holmes **inspects** thoroughly. When others give their **opinions** about who is **guilty**, he gives **facts**. Holmes never falsely accuses an **innocent** person. He is **familiar** with methods of finding criminals that are **unknown** to the police.

Holmes and Watson share a second-story apartment in London. Many **frantic** people **ascend** the stairs to ask for help. By the time the worried person **descends** the stairs, he or she feels **calm** and assured that Holmes can solve the problem.

Sherlock Holmes is an **unusual** character with amazing gifts. His friend Dr. Watson, on the other hand, is more **ordinary**. The two work together very well. They **agree** about most things, but sometimes they **quarrel**. Watson **praises** Holmes for his brilliant mind, but Holmes sometimes **insults** Watson. The great detective thinks Watson allows his emotions to get in the way of his ability to reason or think clearly. Watson, however, has more sympathy for human weakness than the ever-logical Holmes.

The number of Sherlock Holmes fans **expands** every year. Millions have read about his adventures, and millions more may have seen stories about him on television or in movies. Since the interest in detective fiction seems to grow more popular every year, there is little chance that the number of Holmes fans will **shrink** any time soon.

Vocabulary Words

agree	innocent
ascend	inspect
calm	insult
descend	opinion
expand	ordinary
fact	praise
familiar	quarrel
frantic	shrink
glimpse	unknown
guilty	unusual

Word Learning Tip!

An **antonym** is a word that means the opposite or nearly the opposite of another word. Even though their meanings are the opposite, antonyms are always the same part of speech.

Vocabulary Building Strategy

Use Context Clues Clues in the context—the surrounding words and sentences—can help you learn antonyms. The meaning of an antonym is usually found in a phrase or sentence that comes after it and tells the opposite meaning of that word.

10 Antonyms to Know

Connect Words and Meanings

agree	expand	glimpse	insult	quarrel
ascend	fact	guilty	opinion	shrink
calm	familiar	innocent	ordinary	unknown
descend	frantic	inspect	praise	unusual

Directions Read both clues in each item below. Then write the antonyms on the lines in the order that matches the definitions. You may use the glossary to help you.

1. to argue and to share the same ideas

_____

2. to say something good about someone and to say something bad about someone

_____

3. to go up and to go down

_____

4. peaceful and very upset

_____

5. not common and common or everyday

_____

6. unproven information and proven information

_____

7. get larger and get smaller

_____

8. known by a lot of people and not known by anyone

_____

9. to look briefly and to look carefully

_____

10. not having done something wrong and having done something wrong

_____

Connect More Words and Meanings

agree	expand	glimpse	insult	quarrel
ascend	fact	guilty	opinion	shrink
calm	familiar	innocent	ordinary	unknown
descend	frantic	inspect	praise	unusual

Directions Write the letter of the correct vocabulary word on the line next to each definition in the first column.

1. _____ belief or idea

A. glimpse

2. _____ to get smaller

B. ordinary

3. _____ to argue

C. quarrel

4. _____ to say words of approval

D. calm

5. _____ not troubled

E. opinion

6. _____ to move or go up

F. familiar

7. _____ well known and easily recognized

G. shrink

8. _____ to look at briefly

H. innocent

9. _____ not to be blamed

I. praise

10. _____ common or everyday

J. ascend

★ **Make a Chart** Make a chart that shows how two people are opposite. You might choose a superhero or superheroine and contrast him or her with a super-villain. Use five antonyms from the vocabulary list and five new antonyms you find in textbooks, magazines, or newspapers.

Use Words in Context

agree	expand	glimpse	insult	quarrel
ascend	fact	guilty	opinion	shrink
calm	familiar	innocent	ordinary	unknown
descend	frantic	inspect	praise	unusual

Directions Replace the boldface words in each item with a pair of antonyms from the list. Write the replacement words on the blanks after each item.

1. The television detective Columbo is very smart. He has an **extraordinary** intelligence, but he acts like an **everyday** person.

_____ _____

2. Columbo never gets **upset**. No matter what happens, he seems **peaceful**.

_____ _____

3. Detectives working in pairs need to **have the same ideas** on how to solve crimes. If partners **argue**, they lose time and fail to catch the criminals.

_____ _____

4. Columbo and other detectives **look closely at** clues and speak to witnesses. Witnesses who only **briefly see** a suspect are not very helpful.

_____ _____

5. Detectives cannot rely on **beliefs** that are not backed up by evidence. They need to find **true pieces of information** that will hold up in court. (Make the vocabulary words plural.)

_____ _____

6. Sometimes the real criminal is **not known** for a long time. He or she might be a **well-known** person that nobody thinks would ever commit a crime.

_____ _____

7. To gain his suspect's trust, Columbo goes out of his way to **say approving things about** them. He is careful never to **say upsetting things to** his suspects.

_____ _____

8. You would think the pool of criminals would **get smaller** because of great detectives like Columbo, but the numbers of wrongdoers continue to **get bigger** each day—at least on television.

_____ _____

Write a Script Take the chart you created. Partner with a friend to write a television mystery. Write a script for four characters. Describe the setting and action, and create dialogue for your characters. Use at least ten vocabulary words.

Put Words Into Action

agree	expand	glimpse	insult	quarrel
ascend	fact	guilty	opinion	shrink
calm	familiar	innocent	ordinary	unknown
descend	frantic	inspect	praise	unusual

Directions Sort the pairs of antonyms on the vocabulary list. Write the antonyms in the blanks in the sentences where they make the most sense. Do not repeat words.

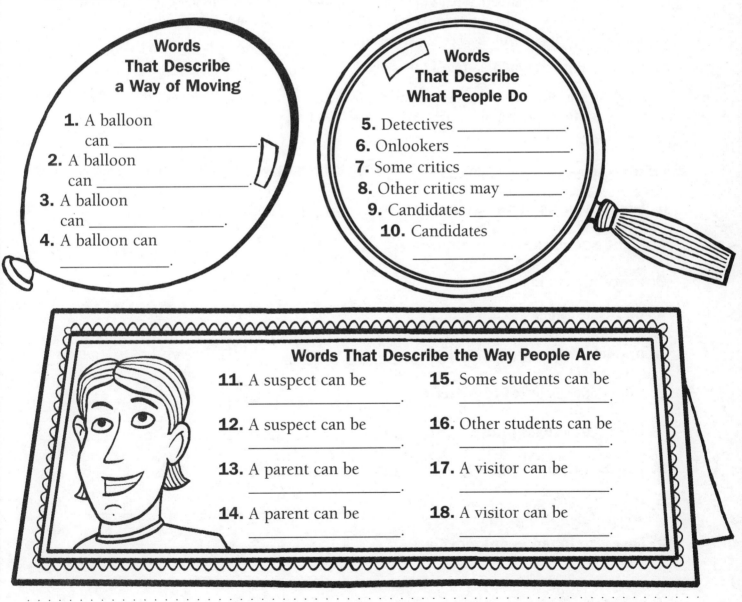

Words That Describe a Way of Moving

1. A balloon can _____.

2. A balloon can _____.

3. A balloon can _____.

4. A balloon can _____.

Words That Describe What People Do

5. Detectives _____.

6. Onlookers _____.

7. Some critics _____.

8. Other critics may _____.

9. Candidates _____.

10. Candidates _____.

Words That Describe the Way People Are

11. A suspect can be _____.

12. A suspect can be _____.

13. A parent can be _____.

14. A parent can be _____.

15. Some students can be _____.

16. Other students can be _____.

17. A visitor can be _____.

18. A visitor can be _____.

Have a Talk Form a small discussion group. Show you know the difference between a fact and an opinion by giving examples of each one using vocabulary words. Then work together to compose a sentence that explains the difference between the two words.

Review and Extend

agree	expand	glimpse	insult	quarrel
ascend	fact	guilty	opinion	shrink
calm	familiar	innocent	ordinary	unknown
descend	frantic	inspect	praise	unusual

Learn More! **Antonyms,** or words that have opposite meanings, can be used in analogies. An **analogy** shows how two pairs of words are related in similar ways. One type of relationship between words is one of opposition or contrast. Here is an example:

Hot is to **cold** as **fast** is to **slow**.

The first pair of words, *hot* and *cold*, are opposites. For the analogy to work, the second pair must have the same relationship.

Directions Complete the analogies below by filling in the correct word from the vocabulary list in the blank.

1. Glance is to **examine** as **glimpse** is to _____.

2. Light is to **dark** as **innocent** is to _____.

3. Peaceful is to **upset** as **calm** is to _____.

4. Rise is to **fall** as **ascend** is to _____.

5. Run is to **walk** as **expand** is to _____.

6. Knowledge is to **belief** as **fact** is to _____.

7. Love is to **hate** as **praise** is to _____.

8. Laugh is to **cry** as **agree** is to _____.

9. Exciting is to **boring** as **unusual** is to _____.

10. Lost is to **found** as **unknown** is to _____.

Write Analogies Work with a partner to create analogies like the ones above. Use at least two sets of antonyms from the vocabulary words. Then write two analogies with antonyms not on the list. Use a dictionary, thesaurus, or glossary to help you.

Check Your Mastery

Directions Fill in the blanks in the items below with words or phrases of your own that show you understand the meaning of the boldface words.

1. If you **insult** people, they will _____ you. If you **praise** them, they will _____ you.

2. You can **ascend** and **descend** on a(n) _____.

3. My stomach will **expand** if I _____, but it will **shrink** again if I _____.

4. A **fact** is _____ while an **opinion** is _____.

5. The student was **frantic** after the _____. She became **calm** when _____.

6. If the man is found **guilty**, he will _____. If the jury believes he is **innocent**, he will _____.

7. When an **unknown** person comes to the door, I _____. If the face is **familiar**, I _____.

8. When friends **quarrel**, they feel _____. When they find a way to **agree**, they feel _____ again.

9. If you **glimpse** at a photograph, you will _____ the details, but if you **inspect** it, you will _____ them.

10. In the state where I live, _____ is **unusual** in the summer but quite **ordinary** in the _____.

Read Words in Context

Vocabulary Words

additionally	lighter
banner	plead
depart	rapid
eastern	retreat
grasp	western

Word Learning Tip!

In this chapter, you have learned that words can be different parts of speech. You can use the part of speech of an unknown word to understand its meaning. Multiple-meaning words have different meanings when they are used as different parts of speech.

Vocabulary Building Strategy

Use Context Clues Context clues can help you determine the meaning of an unfamiliar word. Look for synonyms and antonyms as context clues. Use context clues to understand which meaning of a multiple-meaning word is being used.

 READ!

Lights! Camera! Action!

"Let me explain this scene!" the director calls out.

"Knights are on their way to a tournament, a big event in the Middle Ages. These warriors **depart** from the huge castle of Sir Henry Craft. The sun is rising in the **eastern** sky as they ride on horses in a long line out of the castle gate. Their helpers, called squires, ride in front of the knights. The squires hold up a blue and gold **banner.** This flag shows Sir Henry Craft's colors. In the center there is a special design, called a coat of arms, that also stands for Sir Henry's family name. The knights **grasp** lances in their right hands, and they wear heavy armor that is made of metal plates. **Additionally**, each of them wears a sword on the left side of his armor."

"Everyone moves at a steady, **rapid** pace. The knights ride quickly to get to the tournament on time as the morning sky gets **lighter** and brighter. Finally, they arrive and the event begins. The knights try to knock one another off their horses. Sir Henry falls off his horse. Because knights don't beg, he refuses to **plead** for mercy. Instead he chooses to pay a big fine in gold to the knight who defeated him. Sir Henry decides it's time to **retreat** and withdraws quickly from the tournament."

"The tournament ends as the sun sets in the **western** sky. Everyone is tired after a day of thrilling tournament battles."

"Do you understand the scene?" asks the director. "Okay, let's shoot it now!"

Connect Words and Meanings

additionally	depart	grasp	plead	retreat
banner	eastern	lighter	rapid	western

Directions Match each word with its definition. Write the letter of the correct definition in the blank before the word. You may use the glossary to help you.

1. _____ retreat

A. quick, fast

2. _____ eastern

B. to beg someone to do something

3. _____ banner

C. in addition to, plus, also

4. _____ rapid

D. in or from the west

5. _____ lighter

E. to move back or withdraw from a difficult situation

6. _____ grasp

F. in or from the east

7. _____ western

G. a long piece of cloth with writing, designs, and pictures

8. _____ additionally

H. brighter or less in weight; a device for lighting something

9. _____ depart

I. to hold something tightly

10. _____ plead

J. to leave

(continued on next page)

Connect More Words and Meanings

| additionally | depart | grasp | plead | retreat |
| banner | eastern | lighter | rapid | western |

Directions Use the definition clue to choose the word that fits in each sentence below.

11. A verb that means to beg or to say in court that you are not guilty

The defendant will _____ "not guilty."

12. An adjective that means very fast, quick, or speedy

After the accident, her heartbeat was very _____.

13. An adverb that means in addition to or extra

This summer I would like to go to camp. _____,

I would like to take a trip with my parents to a national park.

14. A noun that names a piece of cloth with a motto or legend

The school proudly displayed the _____ with the words "Reach for the Stars."

15. An antonym pair of adjectives that mean from the east and from the west

Maine is an _____ state, and California is a _____ state.

16. A verb that means to move back from a difficult situation that is also a noun that means a quiet place to go to relax and think

After the soldier was forced to _____,

he went to a _____ to think about what went wrong.

17. A verb that means brighter or less in weight, as well as a noun that means a device for lighting a candle or fire

Josh lit the fire with his _____. After he removed

the cooking supplies, his knapsack was _____.

18. A verb that means to hold something tightly and to understand something

Kim didn't understand. She couldn't _____ the problem.

- -

⭐ **Describe a Medieval Tournament** Work in small groups. Brainstorm different points of view of the lords and ladies who watched the tournament events. Write a description of what they might have seen and how they felt during a tournament. Use at least two vocabulary words and four new verbs in your description.

Use Words in Context

| additionally | depart | grasp | plead | retreat |
| banner | eastern | lighter | rapid | western |

Directions Write the vocabulary word that best fits in the blank.

1. The knight refuses to _____ (*rapid, depart, plead*),

or beg, and quickly offers gold to his enemy.

2. The princess rode slowly east for two days to see the _____

(*eastern, rapid, western*) part of her kingdom.

3. Each knight carried a _____ (*retreat, grasp, banner*)

that had a different design!

4. Lady Elizabeth will _____ (*western, depart, grasp*)

from the castle at 10 A.M. in the morning.

5. Young squires studied all day and, _____

(*eastern, additionally, lighter*), had to learn how to serve food.

6. Lord Henry's horse galloped at a very _____

(*banner, retreat, rapid*) speed and won the race easily.

7. Sir Richard lifted the _____ (*banner, lighter, additionally*)

shield up to his neck, while the squire lifted the heavier one.

8. Lady Katherine told the knights to _____

(*plead, additionally, retreat*) after the attack on the castle.

9. If you travel west, toward the _____ (*eastern, western, lighter*)

kingdoms, you will see Sir Edward Watts's castle.

10. The young squire was told to _____ (*plead, depart, grasp*)

the reins tightly as he rode the horse.

Write a Diary Entry Imagine you are a squire, knight, lord, or lady. Select a vocabulary word that your
character might use from each lesson in this chapter. Put these words in sentences that your
character would write in his or her diary.

Put Words Into Action

| additionally | depart | grasp | plead | retreat |
| banner | eastern | lighter | rapid | western |

Directions Sort the vocabulary words. Write each word under the correct heading. Some words can be used more than once.

Nouns

1. _____

2. _____

3. _____

Verbs

8. _____

9. _____

10. _____

11. _____

Adjectives

4. _____

5. _____

6. _____

7. _____

Adverbs

12. _____

BONUS Choose one noun, one verb, one adjective, and one adverb from the vocabulary words. Write a sentence using all four words.

_____

_____

Become a Play Writer People who write plays know how to write good sentences. See how well you can write directions for a play about a tournament. Write four sentences telling what happens in your play. One sentence will use all the nouns above. One will use all the verbs. One will use all the adjectives. The last will use the adverb.

Review and Extend

additionally	depart	grasp	plead	retreat
banner	eastern	lighter	rapid	western

Learn More!

When you can identify what part of speech an unknown word is, it can help you understand the meaning. You can also use synonyms or antonyms as context clues to help you understand an unfamiliar word by looking for a similar or opposite word that is the same part of speech.

Synonyms and Antonyms

Nancy's team will *leave* at 3 P.M., while Jenny's team will *depart* at 4 P.M.

New Hampshire is an *eastern* state, while Wyoming is a *western* state.

Multiple-meaning words have different meanings when they are used as different parts of speech.

Multiple-Meaning Words

The *lighter* had a strong flame.

A feather is *lighter* than a stone.

Directions Read each sentence. Write what part of speech the boldface word is. Then write a short definition for each word.

The Seven Ups are the number one softball team in the east. They won the championship for the **eastern** division.

1. Part of Speech: _____

2. Definition: _____

The Cougars, on the other hand, are the top softball team in the west. They won the title of **western** champions.

3. Part of Speech: _____

4. Definition: _____

Coach James told the girls that it was important to **grasp** their bats very tightly when it was their turn to hit.

5. Part of Speech: _____

6. Definition: _____

Marissa is the top player for the Seven Ups. **Additionally**, she is the captain of the team.

7. Part of Speech: _____

8. Definition: _____

The **banner** on the gym wall said, "Go Seven Ups! Beat the Cougars!"

9. Part of Speech: _____

10. Definition: _____

 Make a Synonym and Antonym Web Brainstorm synonyms and antonyms for *depart, grasp, plead,* and *rapid.* Think of as many words as possible. You may use a dictionary, thesaurus, and your own knowledge to find these words.

Check Your Mastery

Directions Fill in the blank to complete each sentence.

1. You might see a **banner** at _____.

2. A synonym for **grasp** is _____.

3. One thing you might **plead** for is _____.

4. Most people would **retreat** from _____.

5. An antonym for **rapid** is _____.

6. In the evening, the sun sets in the _____, or in the **western** sky.

7. Another way to say **additionally** is _____.

8. When the word **lighter** describes something that weighs less, it is an _____.

9. The opposite of **western** is _____.

10. A synonym for **depart** is _____.

Words and Their Parts

12 Words With Prefixes (*dis–, fore–, sub–, under–*)

Be a Word Architect

Vocabulary Words

disagreeable	submerge
discomfort	subscription
discontent	subway
displease	subzero
distrust	underground
forearm	underpay
forecaster	underrate
foretell	

Word Learning Tip!

To learn a long word, try looking for the meaning in its parts. Some long words are made up of a prefix and a word or root. A prefix is a letter or group of letters you can add to a word to form a new word. For example, *dis + please = displease*. You can also add a prefix to a root—another word part. For example, the root *merge* comes from the Latin word for "dive": *sub + merge = submerge*.

Vocabulary Building Strategy

Use Prefixes A prefix is always added to the beginning of a word or root. Put together the meaning of the prefix with the meaning of the word or root to determine the meaning of a new word.

Learn More!

A prefix always has the same meaning. Use the meaning of the prefix to help learn what a new word means.

You know something right away about all the words that begin with the prefix *dis–*. They all contain the meaning "not, lack of, or opposite of." Words with the prefix *fore–* all contain the meaning "in front of, ahead of, or before." Words with the prefix *sub–* all contain the meaning "under or lower." Words with the prefix *under–* all contain the meaning "below, beneath, or less than." Notice that the prefixes *sub–* and *under–* mean basically the same thing.

Prefix	Meaning
dis–	not, lack of, opposite of
fore–	in front of, ahead of time, before
sub–	under, lower than
under–	below, beneath, less than

★ **Find New Words With Prefixes** Look through magazines and books. Find at least four new words, one each for the prefixes *dis–*, *fore–*, *sub–*, *under–*. Write the words and the sentences in your journal. Then try to write a new sentence for each word.

Be a Word Architect

disagreeable	displease	forecaster	subscription	underground
discomfort	distrust	foretell	subway	underpay
discontent	forearm	submerge	subzero	underrate

Directions Look at each branch of the prefix tree below. Place each vocabulary word in the blank on the correct branch. Circle the prefix in each word.

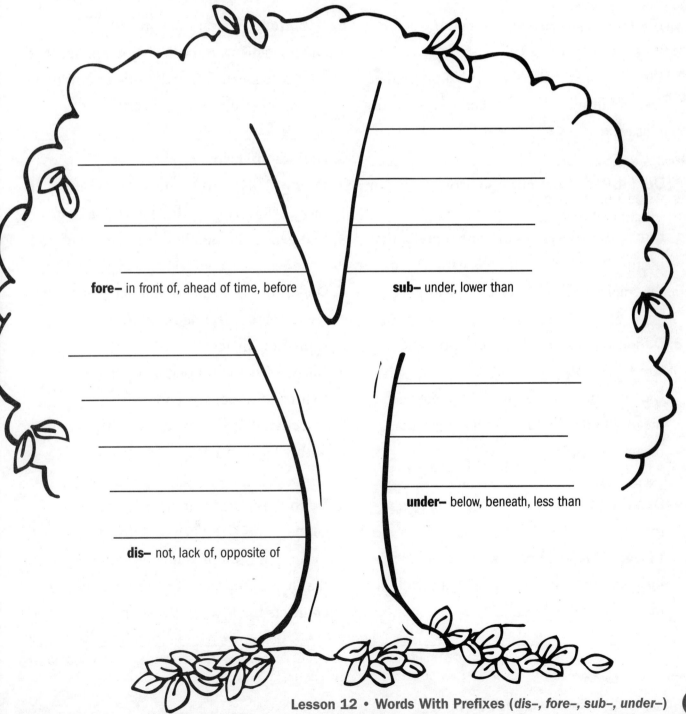

fore– in front of, ahead of time, before

sub– under, lower than

under– below, beneath, less than

dis– not, lack of, opposite of

Connect Words and Meanings

disagreeable	displease	forecaster	subscription	underground
discomfort	distrust	foretell	subway	underpay
discontent	forearm	submerge	subzero	underrate

Directions Read each definition. Then look at the clues. Write the word that matches the definition in the blank. You may use the glossary or a dictionary to help you.

1. Definition: to tell about something before it happens; to predict
Clues: This word begins with a prefix that means "ahead of time." It ends with a verb that means "say."

_____

2. Definition: to not make someone happy or satisfied; to annoy
Clues: This word begins with a prefix that means "opposite of." It ends with a verb that means "to satisfy or give pleasure."

_____

3. Definition: a train that runs under the streets of a city
Clues: This word begins with a prefix that means "under." It ends with a noun that means "a road" or "a route."

_____

4. Definition: to value or judge something too little
Clues: This word begins with a prefix that means "less than." It ends with a verb that means "to judge or rank."

_____

5. Definition: beneath the ground
Clues: This word begins with a prefix that means "beneath." It ends with a noun that means "the surface of the earth."

_____

6. Definition: below zero
Clues: This word begins with a prefix that means "lower than." It ends with a noun that names the number that comes before 1.

_____

7. Definition: a feeling of not being satisfied; restlessness; a feeling of wanting something better
Clues: This word begins with a prefix that means "not." It ends with an adjective that means that you are satisfied with what you have.

_____

8. Definition: the front part of your arm
Clues: This word begins with a prefix that means "in front of." It ends with a noun that names the part of the body that connects the hand to the shoulder.

_____

(continued on next page)

Connect More Words and Meanings

disagreeable	displease	forecaster	subscription	underground
discomfort	distrust	foretell	subway	underpay
discontent	forearm	submerge	subzero	underrate

Directions Continue the activity. Read each definition. Then look at the clues. Write the word that matches the definition in the blank. You may use the glossary or a dictionary to help you.

9. Definition: not trust
Clues: This word begins with a prefix that means "lack of." It ends with a verb that shows that you believe in someone or something.

_____

10. Definition: to pay too little for something or to value something less than it is worth
Clues: This word begins with a prefix that means "less than." It ends with a verb that means "give money in return for something."

_____

11. Definition: pain or worry
Clues: This word begins with a prefix that means "opposite of." It ends with a noun that means "the feeling of being relaxed and free from pain and worry."

_____

12. Definition: not pleasant; not to one's liking
Clues: This word begins with a prefix that means "not." It ends with an adjective that means "pleasant" or "pleasing."

_____

13. Definition: a person who tells what he or she thinks will happen in the future
Clues: This word begins with a prefix that means "ahead of time." It contains the word *cast*, which means "to estimate or guess." It ends with the suffix *-er*, which means "a person who."

_____

14. Definition: to go completely underwater
Clues: This word begins with a prefix that means "under." The second part of the word comes from the Latin word *mergere*, which means "to sink, plunge, or dive."

_____

15. Definition: a signed agreement to receive a magazine or newspaper on a regular basis
Clues: This word begins with a prefix that means "under." The second part of the word comes from the Latin word *scribere*, which means "to write." When you have this, you have written your name under or at the bottom of an agreement to show that you accept what the agreement says.

_____

⭐ **Forecast Future Events** Work in small groups to forecast the future. Talk about events or discoveries that you think might happen in the next 20 years. What will be popular? What will scientists discover? How will people feel about these new discoveries? Then write a paragraph summarizing your discussion. Use as many vocabulary words as you can.

12 Words With Prefixes (*dis–, fore–, sub–, under–*)

Learn Words in Context

disagreeable	displease	forecaster	subscription	underground
discomfort	distrust	foretell	subway	underpay
discontent	forearm	submerge	subzero	underrate

Sam Stormsniffer Tells All

Interviewer: My name is Jenny Jensen. I want to be a weather **forecaster** like you when I grow up, so I'd like to ask you a few questions about your job.

Sam Stormsniffer: I'd be happy to answer your questions, Jenny.

Interviewer: Do you like your job?

Sam Stormsniffer: I like being a forecaster, but in some ways I am **discontent**. For one thing, the TV station **underpays** me. News reporters get much higher pay. That's because weather forecasters are **underrated**. The station owner doesn't think we're that important, but the viewers do. They need our weather reports every day.

Interviewer: Do people **distrust** weather forecasters?

Sam Stormsniffer: Sometimes. Many people don't understand how hard it is to **foretell** the weather. Sometimes what we think will happen doesn't happen. Here's an example. I said that Saturday would be sunny and warm. Unfortunately, it rained all day. It was very **disagreeable** weather, and it **displeased** a lot of people.

Interviewer: What is the worst weather this area has ever had?

Sam Stormsniffer: Last winter, we had **subzero** temperatures with about 40 inches of snow. It caused people a lot of **discomfort**. It wasn't much fun going outdoors. In the spring, all the snow melted in three days and there were floods. It was terrible! Basements of houses were **submerged** in water and so was the **subway**. Workers had to go **underground** and pump out the water. Look at my hand and **forearm.** The water in the subway was up to my elbow.

Interviewer: Wow! That's pretty deep! Well, thank you very much for talking to me. In spite of all the problems, I still really want to become a weather forecaster.

Sam Stormsniffer: Good luck! You may want a **subscription** to *Stormsniffer Weekly*. It's my weekly magazine, which keeps people up to date on weather forecast information. I'll tell you what, how about I give you a free subscription, which saves you $5 a month?

Interviewer: Great! Thanks!

Use Words in Context

disagreeable	displease	forecaster	subscription	underground
discomfort	distrust	foretell	subway	underpay
discontent	forearm	submerge	subzero	underrate

Directions Choose the vocabulary word that fits the definition in boldface. Write the word in the blank.

1. The weather in Alaska is almost always **below zero** in the winter.

_____

2. Some people **do not trust** weather reports.

_____

3. I think that they **rate too low or don't value highly enough** weather scientists.

_____

4. Weather is very hard to **tell ahead of time**.

_____

5. A **person who tells about what will happen in the future** has to read a lot of information.

_____

6. Weather people make mistakes and sometimes **do not please** people.

_____

7. Lucy is tired of the **lack of comfort** during this cold weather.

_____

8. It is **not agreeable or pleasant** to be caught without an umbrella on a rainy day.

_____

9. People are **not content** when they get caught in a rainstorm.

_____

10. Here's one solution to weather problems: Live in a house that is **below the ground**! It's warm in winter and cool in summer.

_____

⭐ **Give a Weather Report** Take a look at some newspaper weather reports. Then work with a partner to write a newspaper weather report for two days. Use symbols for a sunny, rainy, cloudy, or snowy day. Give temperatures and other information. Use at least three vocabulary words in your weather reports.

12 Words With Prefixes (*dis–, fore–, sub–, under–*)

Review and Extend

disagreeable	displease	forecaster	subscription	underground
discomfort	distrust	foretell	subway	underpay
discontent	forearm	submerge	subzero	underrate

NEW WORDS   disappears   discontinue   foreword   subheading   underline

Directions Use what you know about prefixes and other word parts to review the vocabulary and learn new words. Read the sentences. Think about the meaning of the prefix in the boldface word. Then fill in the blank.

1. When divers **submerge**, they go _____ the water.

2. A **subheading** appears _____ the main heading in an article.

3. If you feel **discomfort**, you are _____ at ease.

4. If a store decides to **discontinue** selling an item, they will _____ go on selling it.

5. When scientists **foretell** an earthquake, they say _____ that it will happen.

6. A **foreword** is the words from the author that appear _____ the first chapter in the book.

7. If you **underrate** something, you value it _____ you should.

8. When you **underline** something, you draw a line _____ it.

9. If you **displease** someone, you do the _____ of making that person happy.

10. If someone **disappears**, that person does the _____ of appearing.

BONUS Write a sentence using two of the new vocabulary words. _____

_____

_____

⭐ **Draw a Word Web** Work in small groups. Choose a prefix. On the word web graphic organizer, write your group's prefix in the middle circle. Brainstorm as many new words with this prefix as you can. Write the words and their meanings around the circle. Use a dictionary to find more new words.

Check Your Mastery

Directions Choose the word that best fits each sentence. Write it in the blank.

1. When there is a tornado with high winds, people hide in _____ (*underground, underrate, subzero*) places.

2. Ali decided to get a _____ (*forearm, distrust, subscription*) to a science magazine.

3. Lisa is wearing a bracelet on her _____ (*subway, forearm, submerge*).

4. It is _____ (*disagreeable, underrate, distrust*) to be criticized. Nobody likes it.

5. There was a lot of _____ (*distrust, discontent, foretell*) among the students because it rained so hard the class trip was canceled.

6. We watched the diver _____ (*underground, subscription, submerge*) herself completely under the water.

7. Don't _____ (*underrate, forecaster, discontent*) Vicky's ability. I think she can do the job very well.

8. It was freezing last night. The temperature was _____ (*subzero, underpay, underground*), and the winds were strong.

9. The quickest way to travel in a city is to take the _____ (*underpay, subway, displease*).

10. The weather _____ (*forearm, foretell, forecaster*) said that a storm was coming.

13 Words With Suffixes (–fy, –ic, –ation/–tion, –ment)

Be a Word Architect

Learn More!

Suffix	Meaning	Part of Speech
–fy	to make	verb
–ic	related to or like	adjective
–ation, –tion	the act or state of	noun
–ment	result of an action or state of	noun

Suffixes tell you the part of speech and they give you help in determining the meaning of an unknown word. For example, if you see the word *metallic*, you know from the suffix –*ic* that it is an adjective. Using the meaning of the suffix, you can determine that *metallic* means "related to metal" or "like metal." So something that is *metallic* is probably made of metal. If something has a *metallic* taste, it would taste like metal.

What do the words "state of" mean in the suffix –*ation*, –*tion*, or –*ment*? "State of" tells you that it is the way something is. For example, if you are *fascinated*, you are very interested. *Fascination* is "the state of being fascinated" or the way it feels when you are fascinated.

Vocabulary Words

adjustment	involvement
admiration	magnify
advancement	metallic
application	poetic
extinction	scientific
fascination	simplify
hesitation	terrify
intention	

Word Learning Tip!

Some words are made up of a word or root followed by a suffix. For example, the root *magni–* comes from a Latin word that means "great." A root needs a prefix or suffix to form a word. Add the suffix –*fy* to *magni–* to form *magnify*. When you put together the meanings of the parts, you can figure out the meaning of new words.

Vocabulary Building Strategy

Use Suffixes When you add a suffix to a word, it often changes the part of speech of that word. For example, if you add –*fy* to a word or root, you make a verb. If you add –*ic*, you make an adjective. If you add –*ation*, –*tion*, or –*ment*, you make a noun. Sometimes, there are spelling changes when you add a suffix.

⭐ **Find New Words With Suffixes** Look through newspapers, magazines, or books. Find a new word that contains each of the suffixes in this lesson: –*fy*, –*ic*, –*ation*, –*tion*, –*ment*. Write these words in your personal word journal. Also, write the sentence in which you find each word. Then add them to the suffix tree (page 93).

Be a Word Architect

adjustment	application	hesitation	magnify	scientific
admiration	extinction	intention	metallic	simplify
advancement	fascination	involvement	poetic	terrify

Directions Look at each branch of the suffix tree below. Place each vocabulary word in the blank on the correct branch. Circle the suffix in the word.

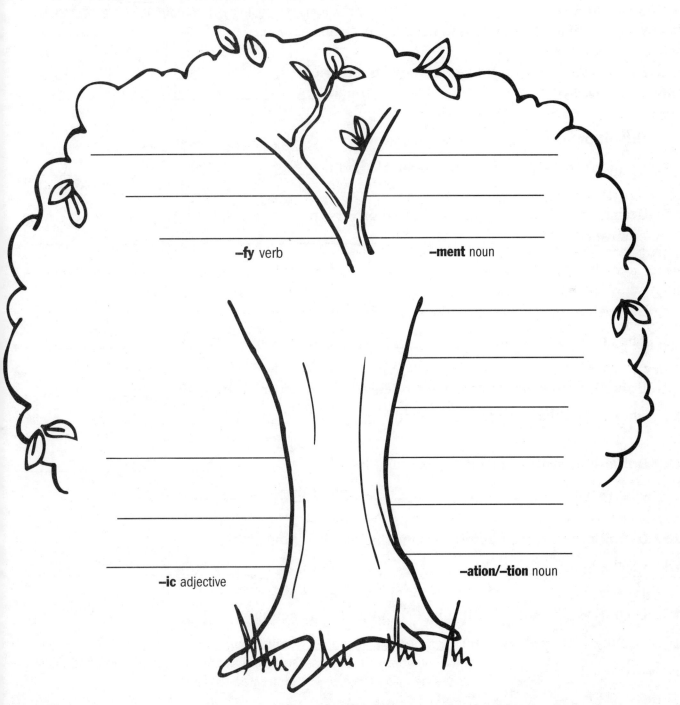

–fy verb

–ment noun

–ic adjective

–ation/–tion noun

Connect Words and Meanings

adjustment	application	hesitation	magnify	scientific
admiration	extinction	intention	metallic	simplify
advancement	fascination	involvement	poetic	terrify

Directions Read each pair of sentences below. Write a vocabulary word that matches each definition by adding a suffix to the word or word part in boldface type. (Some words have spelling changes when you add a suffix. Be sure to check the vocabulary list for the correct spelling.) Then complete the sentence that follows it. You may use the glossary or a dictionary to help you.

1. Definition: like poetry; like the way a **poet** writes _____

2. Someone who is _____ might _____.

3. Definition: the act of **intend**ing or meaning to do something; a plan _____

4. He didn't mean to be late for school. He had no _____ of _____.

5. Definition: the act of being **fascinate**d or very interested in something or someone; strong interest or attraction _____

6. I get a feeling of _____ whenever I _____.

7. Definition: the act of **adjust**ing or moving something a little bit; change _____

8. The tailor had to make an _____ to the pants because _____.

9. Definition: to make someone feel intense fear or **terror**; to frighten _____

10. They hoped that the scarecrow would _____ the _____.

11. Definition: made of **metal** or seeming like metal _____

12. She used a _____ paint to _____.

13. Definition: the act of **admir**ing someone or something; respect _____

14. I feel a lot of _____ for _____.

15. Definition: the act of **hesitat**ing or waiting before acting _____

16. The firefighters showed no _____ before _____.

(continued on next page)

Words With Suffixes (*–fy, –ic, –ation/–tion, –ment*)

Connect More Words and Meanings

adjustment	application	hesitation	magnify	scientific
admiration	extinction	intention	metallic	simplify
advancement	fascination	involvement	poetic	terrify

Directions Continue the activity. Write a vocabulary word that matches each definition by adding a suffix to the word or word part in boldface. Complete the sentence that follows it.

17. Definition: to make something easier or **simpl**er _____

18. In order to _____ the instructions, _____.

19. Definition: a form to fill out to **appl**y for a job or school _____

20. Penelope filled out an _____ for _____.

21. Definition: the act of being included or **involve**d in some activity _____

22. Because of his _____ in the club, _____.

23. Definition: to give something **magni**tude; to make something appear larger with a special glass _____

24. They wanted to _____ the picture so that _____.

25. Definition: something that is concerned with or about **scien**ce _____

26. In my opinion, the most important _____ discovery is the _____.

27. Definition: not existing anymore, or the state of being **extinct** _____

28. The group tries to protect animals and prevent their _____ because _____.

29. Definition: the act or result of **advanc**ing or moving forward; progress _____

30. The general ordered the _____ of the troops so that _____.

Draw a Word Web Write the word *scientific* in the center of a word web. Complete the web by writing all the vocabulary words that may be connected to science. Make sure you can explain how each word is associated with science.

13 Words With Suffixes (–fy, –ic, –ation/–tion, –ment)

Learn Words in Context

adjustment	application	hesitation	magnify	scientific
admiration	extinction	intention	metallic	simplify
advancement	fascination	involvement	poetic	terrify

READ!

Jane Goodall, Scientist

Many scientists have a **fascination** with nature from the time they are children. Bugs and snakes may **terrify** other boys and girls, but not those who have **scientific** minds. They just want to know more about them. They look at bugs and rocks under a microscope. They like to **magnify** things so that they can see small details. For example, if you look at a rock through a magnifying glass, you can see **metallic** bits. Those are pieces of metal in the rock.

Jane Goodall is a scientist who studies chimpanzees in Africa. At the age of ten, Jane told her mother about her **intention** to study animals. Jane said she intended to live in Africa. When Jane was twenty-six, her dream came true when she was asked to work there. Without any **hesitation**, or doubts, she went to Africa to study chimps in the wild.

At first, the chimps were terrified of Jane. Over time, however, they made an **adjustment** to her. They began to trust her and let her come closer to them. Jane's **involvement** with the chimps helped her learn many surprising facts about them.

A famous scientist felt a lot of **admiration** for Jane. He helped her make an **application** to study higher-level science at college. This led to her **advancement** in the world of science. Jane used her fame to help the chimps. She worked hard to save them from **extinction** because she believed chimps were too important to let them no longer exist.

Jane Goodall has written many books about chimps. She writes in a **poetic** way about her love of animals. She can **simplify** scientific ideas so that most people can understand them easily.

Use Words in Context

adjustment	application	hesitation	magnify	scientific
admiration	extinction	intention	metallic	simplify
advancement	fascination	involvement	poetic	terrify

Directions Choose the word that best completes each sentence. Write the word in the blank.

1. Many scientists are worried about the _____ (*intention, extinction, advancement*) of animals in the wild. Animals such as tigers and pandas are few in number.

2. A lot of people work hard to protect animals. Their _____ (*adjustment, fascination, involvement*) in the fight to save animals has had many good results. Scientists are glad that so many people are involved.

3. Laws have been passed to protect wild animals. The _____ (*intention, poetic, metallic*) of these laws is to keep these animals alive and to protect the places where they live.

4. When I was asked to fill out an _____ (*application, simplify, adjustment*) for the job, I quickly agreed. I really wanted to work for an organization that helps animals.

Directions Read each question. Use the word in boldface in your answer. Write your sentence in the blank.

5. Name a person for whom you have a lot of **admiration**. Tell why you admire this person.

_____

6. Name a **scientific** topic that interests you. Tell why it interests you.

_____

7. Name something that might **terrify** you. Tell why it might terrify you.

_____

8. Name something that you would like to **magnify** under a magnifying glass. Tell why you would like to magnify it. _____

⭐ **Discuss Animal Scientists** Work in small groups. Imagine that you are a scientist who studies animals in the wild. Think about the qualities a person would need to live in the wild and study wild animals. Use as many words ending in *-fy, -ic, -ation, -tion,* and *-ment* as you can in your discussion. Keep track of these words by writing them and their meanings in your personal word journal.

13 Words With Suffixes (–fy, –ic, –ation/–tion, –ment)

Review and Extend

adjustment	application	hesitation	magnify	scientific
admiration	extinction	intention	metallic	simplify
advancement	fascination	involvement	poetic	terrify

NEW WORDS   magnification   simplification

Directions Use the suffixes –ment, –ation, or –tion to turn each boldface verb into a noun. Write the noun in the blank. (There may be some spelling change when you add the suffix.)

1. A sunset has the power to **fascinate** me. I feel a sense of _____ when I watch a sunset.

2. Kim wanted to **involve** his parents in planning the party. He wanted their _____.

3. The football player tried to **advance** with the ball. His _____ was stopped by the other team.

4. The doctor tried to **adjust** Leticia's glasses. Her glasses needed an _____.

5. Tito knew the answer and did not **hesitate** before responding. He showed no _____.

6. I **admire** people who work hard to make this a better world. They fill me with _____.

7. Carmen wants to **apply** to that camp. Her parents will help her fill out an _____.

8. Do you **intend** to try out for the school band? What is your _____ ?

9. The scientist uses a microscope to **magnify** the image. _____ makes the image easier to see.

10. The teacher tried to **simplify** the problem. Her _____ made it easier to solve.

⭐ **Guess My Word** Work with a partner. Each of you should choose a vocabulary word and write it in your personal word journal. Then take turns asking each other questions about the word. Challenge each other to guess the other's word in as few turns as possible.

Check Your Mastery

Directions Read each item below. Circle the letter of the word that best fits in the sentence.

1. This is what you do when you study nature. You study something in a _____ way.
   A. simplify   **B.** scientific   **C.** fascination

2. If you read only books about lions, then you probably have a _____ with this animal.
   A. hesitation   **B.** advancement   **C.** fascination

3. A microscope makes tiny things much bigger. It can _____ a bug so that you can see the bug in great detail.
   A. magnify   **B.** simplify   **C.** metallic

4. You fill out an _____ form in order to get a job. On this form, you tell information about yourself.
   A. application   **B.** involvement   **C.** extinction

5. Often, Jim means to do something good, such as help with chores. His _____ is good, but he may not get around to doing it.
   A. poetic   **B.** intention   **C.** adjustment

6. Mrs. Garcia tried to make the difficult mathematics problem easier for her students. She tried to _____ the idea so that they could understand it.
   A. involvement   **B.** simplify   **C.** scientific

7. It is usually difficult to move to a new town. You must make a big _____ to a new school and classmates.
   A. terrify   **B.** intention   **C.** adjustment

8. If tigers die out, they will be gone forever. The _____ of any group of animals upsets the natural balance in the world of nature.
   A. terrify   **B.** extinction   **C.** admiration

9. Louisa was very happy when she got the promotion at work. The _____ meant that she had more people working for her and more responsibilities.
   A. advancement   **B.** magnify   **C.** scientific

10. Poets often express a love of nature in their poems. Their _____ words often help readers see nature in new and different ways.
    A. application   **B.** simplify   **C.** poetic

14 Words With Common Roots (aster/astro, stel/stell, mar/mari, mig/migr)

Be a Word Architect

Vocabulary Words

aquamarine	emigrate
aster	immigrate
asterisk	marina
astronaut	maritime
astronomer	migrate
astronomical	stellar
astronomy	submarine
constellation	

Word Learning Tip!

You can learn the meaning of many long words if you know the meanings of any of the parts in them. These parts give clues that will help you determine the meaning of the entire word.

Vocabulary Building Strategy

Use Roots A root is a word part that carries a word's main meaning. A root cannot stand by itself as a word. It needs a prefix, suffix, or another root or word added to it to form a word. To determine the meaning of a word with a root, add the meaning of the root together with the meaning of any prefixes or suffixes in the word. For example, *astro* means "star": *astro + naut = astronaut*. An *astronaut* is a traveler to the stars and space.

Learn More!

Root	Meaning
aster/astro	star, of the stars
stel/stell	star, starlike
mar/mari	sea, of the sea or ships
mig/migr	to move

When you see a word with the root *aster/astro* or *stel/stell*, you know that it has something to do with stars. When you see a word with the root *mar/mari*, you know it tells about the sea or ships. When you see a word *mig/migr*, you know it has to do with moving. The meaning of these roots is a great aid that helps you determine the meaning of unfamiliar words.

Find New Words Work with a partner to find other words with the roots in the chart on this page. Try to find one new word for each root. Check your words in the dictionary. Write each word with its meaning in your personal word journal and underline the root.

Words With Common Roots (*aster/astro, stel/stell, mar/mari, mig/migr*)

Be a Word Architect

aquamarine	astronomer	emigrate	migrate
aster	astronomical	immigrate	stellar
asterisk	astronomy	marina	submarine
astronaut	constellation	maritime	

Directions Look at the root tree below. Place each vocabulary word on the correct branch of the tree. Circle the root in each word.

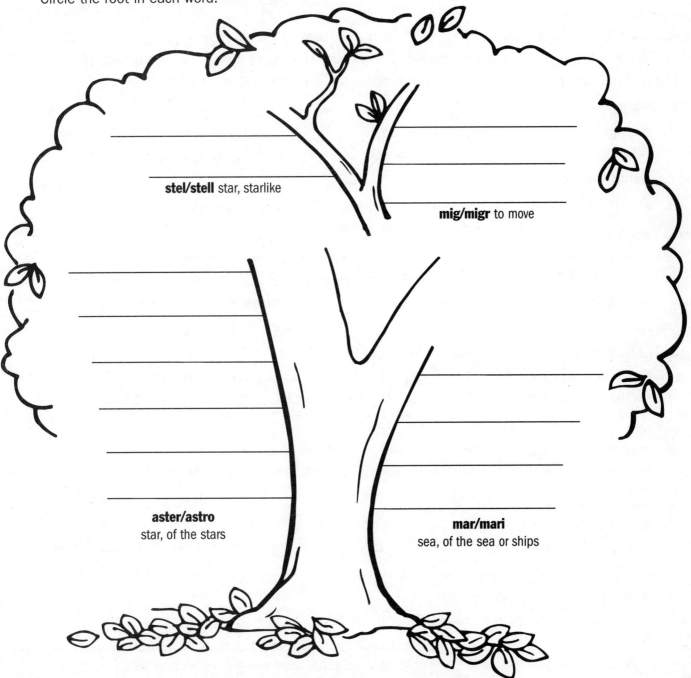

stel/stell star, starlike

mig/migr to move

aster/astro
star, of the stars

mar/mari
sea, of the sea or ships

14 **Words With Common Roots** (*aster/astro, stel/stell, mar/mari, mig/migr*)

Connect Words and Meanings

aquamarine	astronomer	emigrate	migrate
aster	astronomical	immigrate	stellar
asterisk	astronomy	marina	submarine
astronaut	constellation	maritime	

Directions Read each definition below. Then answer the question that follows each definition. Write your answer on the line. Use the vocabulary word in your answer.

1. **constellation:** a group of stars that form a pattern in the sky
   The Big Dipper is a **constellation** of seven stars that form a bowl with a handle. How can this constellation that points to the North Star help sailors navigate? _____
   _____

2. **immigrate:** to come into a country to stay
   Why do you think people would leave the country in which they were born and **immigrate** to a new country? _____

3. **astronomer:** a scientist who studies the stars, planets, and space
   What is one question that an **astronomer** might try to answer? _____
   _____

4. **submarine:** a ship that can travel both on the surface of the ocean and underwater
   How do you think it would feel to be a sailor on a **submarine**? _____
   _____

5. **asterisk:** a star-shaped symbol
   If you see an **asterisk** next to a word in a book you are reading, you look at the bottom of the page. What is the symbol next to the footnote called and what shape would it have?
   _____

6. **maritime:** having to do with ships, sailors, and the sea
   If you read a book about **maritime** history, what would you be reading about?
   _____

7. **stellar:** relating to or being like a star; outstanding
   What performance have you seen in a movie or on television that you would describe as **stellar**? _____

8. **emigrate:** to leave a country for good
   What could make people **emigrate** from the country where they were born and raised?
   _____

(continued on next page)

Connect More Words and Meanings

aquamarine	astronomer	emigrate	migrate
aster	astronomical	immigrate	stellar
asterisk	astronomy	marina	submarine
astronaut	constellation	maritime	

Directions Continue this activity. Read each definition below. Then answer the question that follows each definition. Write your answer on the line.

9. aster: a star-shaped flower with petals around a yellow center

How is an **aster** different from a rose? _____

10. marina: a place to leave a boat; a small harbor where boats are kept

What is one reason that someone might leave a boat in a **marina**? _____

_____

11. astronaut: a traveler to the stars; someone who travels in space

Why do you think that an **astronaut** needs to be brave? _____

_____

12. aquamarine: the blue-green color of the sea; a gemstone that is a blue-green color

Would you like your bedroom to be painted **aquamarine**? Why or why not?

_____

13. astronomical: having to do with the stars or their study; very large

What do you think a group of **astronomical** instruments are used for?

_____

14. migrate: to move from place to place, usually at fixed times

If you are studying how birds **migrate** in the spring and in the fall, what are you

learning about? _____

15. astronomy: the scientific study of the stars

What subjects in school should you try to learn a lot about if you want to enter the field

of **astronomy**? _____

Write Sentences With a partner, choose three vocabulary words with the same root and write sentences using these words. Make sure your sentences show that you know what the words mean.

14 Words With Common Roots (aster/astro, stel/stell, mar/mari, mig/migr)

Learn Words in Context

aquamarine	astronomer	emigrate	migrate
aster	astronomical	immigrate	stellar
asterisk	astronomy	marina	submarine
astronaut	constellation	maritime	

READ!

Daydreaming

It was September. The white and purple **asters** were in bloom. Luis sat on the dock of the **marina**. The sun was shining brightly on the **aquamarine** water. The sunlight on the waves sparkled like silver **asterisks**. Sailboats passed by quietly as if in a dream.

The boats made Luis think of the sailors of long ago. These sailors saw pictures or patterns in the stars in the night sky. The sailors of long ago used these star patterns to steer their boats across the open ocean. These clusters of stars came to be called **constellations**. The sailors gave names to the stars. A group of stars might look like a bear or a man with a bow and arrow.

Sometimes Luis thought he wanted to become an **astronomer.** Then he could learn all about the stars, planets, and other heavenly bodies. Maybe he would even invent an **astronomical** device that would advance the science of **astronomy**. Or, he could become an **astronaut** and travel into space.

If he couldn't go to outer space, perhaps he could have a **maritime** career and travel the waterways of the earth. He could work on a huge container ship or an oil tanker or maybe under the sea in a **submarine**. A career as a naval officer would be a **stellar** adventure. Everyone would admire him, and he could travel all around the world. He could **migrate** easily from country to country. When he retired from the navy, he could move wherever he wanted. Perhaps by that time he could **immigrate** to a colony on the Moon or Mars. Or he could stay in the United States if he did not want to **emigrate.** He would have the knowledge to make the best possible choice for himself.

Suddenly, Luis realized the sun was setting and he had spent the afternoon dreaming about his future. It was time to return to the present and go home for dinner.

Use Words in Context

aquamarine	astronomer	emigrate	migrate
aster	astronomical	immigrate	stellar
asterisk	astronomy	marina	submarine
astronaut	constellation	maritime	

Directions Replace the underlined words with a vocabulary word. Write the vocabulary word in the blank at the beginning of each item.

1. _____ Viktor decided to <u>leave his own country</u> because he could not find a job.

2. _____ The sailors met at the <u>place where boats are kept</u> before the race.

3. _____ The coach was proud of the <u>brilliant, starlike</u> performance of the gymnastics team.

4. _____ Thousands of people <u>move permanently</u> to the United States every year.

5. _____ I like to read books about <u>the science of the stars and planets</u>.

6. _____ Maria Mitchell discovered a comet in 1847. She was the first American woman to become a(n) <u>scientist who studies the stars and planets</u>.

7. _____ Sailors long ago gave names to the <u>groups of stars</u> they saw in the sky.

8. _____ The child placed a single <u>star-shaped flower</u> in a tiny vase.

9. _____ Elisa's dress is <u>blue-green in color</u>, like the sea on a sunny day.

10. _____ A(n) <u>ship that travels underwater</u> can't be seen by ships that are traveling on the top of the water.

 Make a Poster Work with a partner to create a poster that invites people to move to the United States. First, write a short sentence of invitation using the word *immigrate*. Then write three or four sentences telling about good features of American life. Find or draw a picture to illustrate your poster that sends the message that this is a great place to live.

14 Words With Common Roots (aster/astro, stel/stell, mar/mari, mig/migr)

Review and Extend

aquamarine	astronomer	emigrate	migrate
aster	astronomical	immigrate	stellar
asterisk	astronomy	marina	submarine
astronaut	constellation	maritime	

NEW WORDS   asteroid   disaster   migrant   mariner   astrodome

Directions Read the definition of each new word. Then answer the question that follows. Use both boldface words in your response.

1. **asteroid:** a very small planet that travels around the sun

   How could an **astronomer** study an **asteroid**? _____

   _____

2. **mariner:** a sailor

   What stories might a **mariner** tell while his boat is docked in a **marina**? _____

   _____

3. **disaster:** an event that causes great damage or loss

   Note the root *aster* in *disaster*. Long ago, people thought evil stars brought disaster. They looked at the position of stars and **constellations** to predict good fortune or **disaster**. If the stars seemed to be in a bad position, what types of disasters might these people predict?

   _____

4. **astrodome:** a clear dome or roof shaped like half a ball on a building or aircraft used for navigation or finding the way

   Why would **astrological** equipment be kept in the **astrodome**? _____

   _____

5. **migrant:** someone or something that moves from place to place

   Would a **migrant** worker be more likely to stay in one place or to **migrate** from place to place? Why?

   _____

⭐ **Write a Space Adventure** English is constantly growing, with new words formed to describe new situations and new things. Write a story about an adventure for an *astrodog*, a dog that lives in space. Use your knowledge of word parts to form at least three new words. Use at least three of your vocabulary words, too.

Words With Common Roots (aster/astro, stel/stell, mar/mari, mig/migr)

Check Your Mastery

Directions Complete each sentence below. Write your answer in the blanks.

1. **Astronomy** is the science of studying the _____.

2. At a **marina,** you will see _____.

3. If a painting is mostly **aquamarine**, it has a lot of _____.

4. The reward for a **stellar** performance at the Olympics is a(n) _____.

5. A **constellation** of stars forms _____.

Directions Choose the best word to replace the underlined words in each sentence.
Circle the letter of your choice.

6. In 1983, Guion Bluford became the first African American <u>traveler in space</u>.

   A. constellation   **B.** astronaut   **C.** immigrate

7. If you see a(n) <u>mark that looks like a star</u> at the end of a sentence, look for a footnote at the bottom of the page.

   A. aster   **B.** aquamarine   **C.** asterisk

8. Some animals <u>move from place to place</u> when the weather changes.

   A. maritime   **B.** migrate   **C.** emigrate

9. The Hubble telescope is a modern <u>star-studying</u> device.

   A. astronomical   **B.** submarine   **C.** constellation

10. We visited a waterfront museum that focused on <u>shipping by sea</u> history.

   A. astronaut   **B.** astronomy   **C.** maritime

Be a Word Architect

Vocabulary Words

barefoot	runway
crossroads	safeguard
downpour	spotlight
flashlight	teammate
folklore	thunderstorm
lifeguard	timetable
loudspeaker	videotape
masterpiece	

Word Learning Tip!

A compound word is made up of two words that are put together to make one new word. If you know the meaning of the words that make up a compound word, you can determine the meaning of the whole word.

Vocabulary Building Strategy

Use Compound Words When you come across a long word that you do not know, look to see if it contains individual words that make it up. Then you should think about what the individual words mean. Next, add the meanings of the individual words together to come up with a meaning for the compound word. Finally, check to see if that meaning makes sense in the context in which you found the compound word.

Directions Read each compound word. Draw a line or slash between the two words that make up the compound word. Then write the two words in the blanks.

1. barefoot _____ _____

2. videotape _____ _____

3. downpour _____ _____

4. timetable _____ _____

5. folklore _____ _____

6. loudspeaker _____ _____

7. thunderstorm _____ _____

8. runway _____ _____

9. teammate _____ _____

10. spotlight _____ _____

11. crossroads _____ _____

12. flashlight _____ _____

13. lifeguard _____ _____

14. masterpiece _____ _____

15. safeguard _____ _____

⭐ **Write a Sentence** Choose one of the compound words from the vocabulary list. Break it apart into the two words that formed it. Write a sentence using each of these words. Then do the same thing for three additional vocabulary words.

Connect Words and Meanings

barefoot	flashlight	loudspeaker	safeguard	thunderstorm
crossroads	folklore	masterpiece	spotlight	timetable
downpour	lifeguard	runway	teammate	videotape

Directions Read each definition. Put the boldface words together to form a compound word that fits each definition. Then read the sentence that follows. Write this compound word in the first blank and then complete the sentence.

1. **Definition:** heavy rains that **pour down**

   During a sudden _____, I might _____.

2. **Definition:** the place where two **roads cross** one another; a point where two directions are possible.

   At a _____, you might find a sign that says _____.

3. **Definition:** a **storm** with **thunder** and lightning

   During a _____, you might _____.

4. **Definition:** a **table** telling the **time** of arrivals and departures; a schedule

   You might find a _____ on the wall at a _____.

5. **Definition:** a **tape** on which **video** or images are recorded

   We made a _____ of _____.

6. **Definition:** a **mate** or fellow member of a **team**

   When you pass a ball to a _____, you hope that _____.

7. **Definition:** the **lore**, or customs, stories, and beliefs, of the **folk**, or common people; knowledge or beliefs passed down from people to people

   My favorite character from _____ is _____.

8. **Definition:** a **piece** of work or art by a **master** or expert; an outstanding piece of work

   If a museum has a _____ by an artist, it has _____.

(continued on next page)

15 Compound Words

Connect More Words and Meanings

barefoot	flashlight	loudspeaker	safeguard	thunderstorm
crossroads	folklore	masterpiece	spotlight	timetable
downpour	lifeguard	runway	teammate	videotape

Directions Continue this activity. Read each definition and put the boldface words together to form a compound word that fits the definition. Then read the sentence that follows. Write this compound word in the first blank and then complete the sentence.

9. **Definition:** without any covering on the feet; one **foot** and the other **foot** are **bare**

   It's fun to walk _____ when _____.

10. **Definition:** a **light** that you can **flash** on and off; a small, battery-powered lighting device

    I need a _____ when _____.

11. **Definition:** a person who is trained to **guard** the **life** of a person who is swimming; a person trained to save swimmers in danger

    The _____ blew her whistle when she _____.

12. **Definition:** a device that turns electric signals into sounds and makes the voice of the **speaker loud** enough to be heard over a large area

    The coach spoke over the _____ in order to _____.

13. **Definition:** a strip of ground, path, or **way** where aircraft seem to make a **run** for the sky, then take off and later land; a narrow walkway on a stage

    The plane couldn't take off because the _____ was _____.

14. **Definition:** something that serves as a **guard** or to keep things **safe**; to protect someone

    The balcony has a railing as a _____ to make sure that _____.

15. **Definition:** a beam of **light** that shines on a certain **spot** or area

    The _____ showed the two actors _____.

⭐ **Describe a Masterpiece** In your personal word journal, describe something you have seen or heard that you think is a masterpiece. What is it? Why do you like it? Try to use at least three vocabulary words and one other compound word in your description.

Learn Words in Context

barefoot	flashlight	loudspeaker	safeguard	thunderstorm
crossroads	folklore	masterpiece	spotlight	timetable
downpour	lifeguard	runway	teammate	videotape

READ!

What a Party!

For more than 50 years, our city has sponsored a yearly party at the lake. Stories about this party have become part of our **folklore**. Just about everyone has heard tales about this party as they were growing up, and they in turn have told them to their children.

This year's party was a big success. Buses took people to and from the beach throughout the day. There was a published **timetable** so people could find out exactly when the buses traveled.

One of the most popular activities was the sandcastle contest. Albert Yeh created a fantasy home of the future. It even had a **runway** for a plane to land on. He beamed with pride as the newspaper photographer took a picture of him and his **masterpiece**. Albert likes attention, and he was in the **spotlight.**

Two teams competed in a game of volleyball. The team members played **barefoot** on the sand. At one point, one **teammate** hit the ball so hard that it ended up in a big, dark hole. Someone had to get a **flashlight** to see where it had gone.

In the late afternoon, huge clouds formed and the wind picked up. The **lifeguard** said it looked as if a **thunderstorm** was approaching. She wanted to **safeguard** swimmers from any danger, so she called out over her **loudspeaker**, "Everyone out of the water!" Everybody got out quickly and ran for shelter just as the **downpour** began.

Inside the picnic tent, the mayor spoke to us all. A news reporter made a **videotape** of his speech. "Our city is a great place to live, but it is now at a **crossroads**. As we get bigger, we may be tempted to forget our traditions. We must never lose the spirit shown here today."

15 Compound Words

Use Words in Context

barefoot	flashlight	loudspeaker	safeguard	thunderstorm
crossroads	folklore	masterpiece	spotlight	timetable
downpour	lifeguard	runway	teammate	videotape

Directions Choose the best vocabulary word to fit in each blank. Write your answer on the line.

1. The mayor announced that piles of snow were blocking the _____ (*runway, timetable, lifeguard*), so the airport was closed.

2. He said that the museum has bought a _____ (*spotlight, downpour, masterpiece*) by the great artist Frida Kahlo.

3. The mayor reported that the children had received flu vaccines to _____ (*safeguard, loudspeaker, teammate*) them against the illness.

4. He announced an outing to our famous caves. The city would supply _____ (*flashlights, loudspeakers, videotapes*) to help people explore them.

5. The mayor made an announcement over the _____ (*folklore, loudspeaker, masterpiece*).

6. A _____ (*barefoot, safeguard, lifeguard*) would be stationed at each pool to watch the swimmers.

7. "Visit our parks in the summer," he said. "Take a walk _____ (*downpour, barefoot, timetable*) through the grass."

8. The _____ (*teammate, spotlight, loudspeaker*) shone on the mayor as he stood on the platform. It lit up his face.

9. "In the past," he said, "most _____ (*videotape, crossroads, folklore*) was passed on by word of mouth and not written down."

10. "Now we will form teams of people to collect our stories. Each person will work with a partner, or _____ (*lifeguard, teammate, barefoot*)."

⭐ **Write About Teamwork** Just like the word *teammate*, the word *teamwork* also contains the smaller word *team*. Teamwork is when people work together for a common goal. In your personal word journal, tell whether you think teamwork is important or not. Use at least three vocabulary words and one new compound word.

Review and Extend

barefoot	flashlight	loudspeaker	safeguard	thunderstorm
crossroads	folklore	masterpiece	spotlight	timetable
downpour	lifeguard	runway	teammate	videotape

NEW WORDS   bareheaded   downside   lightweight   thunderclap   timeline

Directions Use one of your vocabulary words or a new compound word to answer each question. The boldface clue will help you choose the correct word.

1. What do you look for when the power fails and the **lights** go out?

_____

2. A **light** jacket that you would wear in the spring is made of what type of material?

_____

3. What can you use to find out what **time** a train will come?

_____

4. If you wanted to show events in the order in which they happened in **time**, you might display them on what?

_____

5. What happens when the rain comes **down** suddenly and surprises you?

_____

6. Everyone goes through "ups and **downs**," or good times and bad times. If you look at only the bad points, what do you look at?

_____

7. What word describes your feet when you take off your shoes, **bare** your feet, and walk on the grass?

_____

8. A doctor will tell you not to go out in the rain without a hat or scarf to cover your **head**. How shouldn't you go out?

_____

9. What kind of **storm** sometimes frightens children and dogs because of the noise and lightning? _____

10. What sound might you hear when it **thunders**?

_____

⭐ **Find More New Words** With a partner, make a list of the shorter words that make up each new compound word. Then work together to come up with more compound words made from these individual words. Try to write a definition of each new compound word in your personal word journal.

Check Your Mastery

Directions Complete each sentence in a way that shows you understand the boldface word. Write your answer on the line.

1. You might need a **flashlight** when _____.

2. If you get caught in a **downpour**, you may want to _____.

3. **Lifeguards** have to be good swimmers because _____.

4. One thing you can find on a train **timetable** is _____.

5. A danger of walking **barefoot** is _____.

Directions Circle the word choice that correctly completes each item.

6. Greg stopped at the _____. He did not know which way to turn.

    spotlight   **crossroads**   **barefoot**

7. Folktales about Anansi the Spider are part of African _____.

    videotape   **folklore**   **spotlight**

8. We watched a _____ of my cousin's wedding.

    masterpiece   **timetable**   **videotape**

9. There was a lot of lightning during yesterday's _____.

    thunderstorm   **masterpiece**   **loudspeaker**

10. The basketball player tossed the ball to his _____.

    safeguard   **teammate**   **runway**

Be a Word Architect

Learn More!

Each of the vocabulary words is built from the word *care*. Knowing the meaning of a prefix or suffix will help you determine the meaning of the new word. (Note: When you add a suffix beginning with a vowel to *care*, you drop the *e* at the end of *care*. For example: *care + ing = caring*)

Prefix	Suffix
un– *not*	**–er** *a person who*
	–ful *full of*
	–ing *action of*
	–less *without, lacking*
	–ly *in a certain way*
	–ness *state or quality of (makes a noun)*

Also, some words are compound words made from other words and words plus suffixes: *carefree, caregiver, caretaker, childcare, daycare,* and *healthcare*. Knowing the meaning of each word in the compound will help you learn the meaning of the compound word.

Vocabulary Words

carefree	caretaker
careful	caring
carefully	childcare
carefulness	daycare
caregiver	healthcare
careless	uncaring
carelessly	uncaringly
carelessness	

Word Learning Tip!

Words can have similar meanings when they all contain the same smaller word. Longer words with the same words in them can be grouped together as a word family, since the meanings are related. In this lesson, you will study the word family based on the word *care*.

Vocabulary Building Strategy

Understand Word Families
Some words are related because they have the same word in them. If you know the meaning of this main word in a word family, it can help you figure out the meaning of all the larger words.

Write About a Proverb Many proverbs tell us to be careful. One English proverb says, "Look before you leap." An Italian one says, "The stitch is lost unless the thread is knotted." Choose one of these or another proverb about being careful. Write what you think it means, and tell whether or not you agree with it. Use at least four vocabulary words.

Be a Word Architect

carefree	carefulness	carelessly	caring	healthcare
careful	caregiver	carelessness	childcare	uncaring
carefully	careless	caretaker	daycare	uncaringly

Directions Look at each word below. Try to determine the word parts that make it up. Then write each word in the correct box.

Care + one suffix

1. _____
2. _____
3. _____

Care + word

10. _____

Care + two suffixes

4. _____
5. _____
6. _____
7. _____

Care + word + suffix

11. _____
12. _____

Prefix + *Care* + one or more suffixes

8. _____
9. _____

Word + *Care*

13. _____
14. _____
15. _____

Connect Words and Meanings

carefree	carefulness	carelessly	caring	healthcare
careful	caregiver	carelessness	childcare	uncaring
carefully	careless	caretaker	daycare	uncaringly

Directions Read each definition below. Then use your knowledge of word parts to write the correct vocabulary word in the blanks. You may use your dictionary or the glossary to help you.

1. **Definition:** state or quality of being careful; giving close attention to one's work

   By showing a little _____ when you begin a project, you can avoid a lot of problems.

2. **Definition:** taking great care while doing something

   Belinda is very _____ when she does her mathematics homework.

3. **Definition:** the care given to prevent and treat illness

   The clinic offered classes in _____ to its patients.

4. **Definition:** showing care or concern

   In her speech, Senator Bartelli said that we needed to be a more _____ society.

5. **Definition:** not giving close attention to what one is doing; done without care

   In some jobs, being _____ can cause injuries.

6. **Definition:** having no interest or sympathy; lacking affection; without care or thought for others

   Senator Chin argued that the other candidate was _____ and showed no concern for others.

7. **Definition:** in a way that shows little care, affection, or thought for others

   The nurses treat the patients in a very caring way. They do not treat the patients

   _____.

8. **Definition:** in a way that shows little thought or care and that often leads to mistakes

   If you add up the numbers _____, you will make mistakes.

(continued on next page)

Connect More Words and Meanings

carefree	carefulness	carelessly	caring	healthcare
careful	caregiver	carelessness	childcare	uncaring
carefully	careless	caretaker	daycare	uncaringly

Directions Continue this activity. Read each definition below. Then use your knowledge of word parts to write the correct vocabulary word in the blank in each sentence. You may use your dictionary or the glossary to help you.

9. **Definition:** done in a way that shows or takes great care

   When Tony helps his brother in the tool shop, he works very _____.

10. **Definition:** state or quality of not being careful or not giving close attention to what one is doing

   The carpenter kept making mistakes. His _____ lost him his job.

11. **Definition:** care given during the day to very young children away from their homes; place where care is provided

   Some businesses provide _____ for the young children of their employees.

12. **Definition:** person employed to look after goods, property, or a person

   The _____ took care of the grounds while the owners were away.

13. **Definition:** without any worries or care; free from care

   During the summer, Amelia felt _____ and without worries.

14. **Definition:** a person who gives care to sick people or who attends to needs of a child; a doctor or nurse

   When Mr. Johnston took ill, the doctor asked who the _____ or person providing care would be.

15. **Definition:** of, relating to, or providing care for children

   The new parents bought a book about _____.

Write About a Caring Job In your personal word journal, write a paragraph about something you have to take care of. For example, it could be a pet, a plant, your room, your toys, your books, a school project, or a community activity. Use at least five vocabulary words in your paragraph.

Learn Words in Context

carefree	carefulness	carelessly	caring	healthcare
careful	caregiver	carelessness	childcare	uncaring
carefully	careless	caretaker	daycare	uncaringly

Nick's big brother Kevin was looking for his first job. He read the want ads in the local paper.

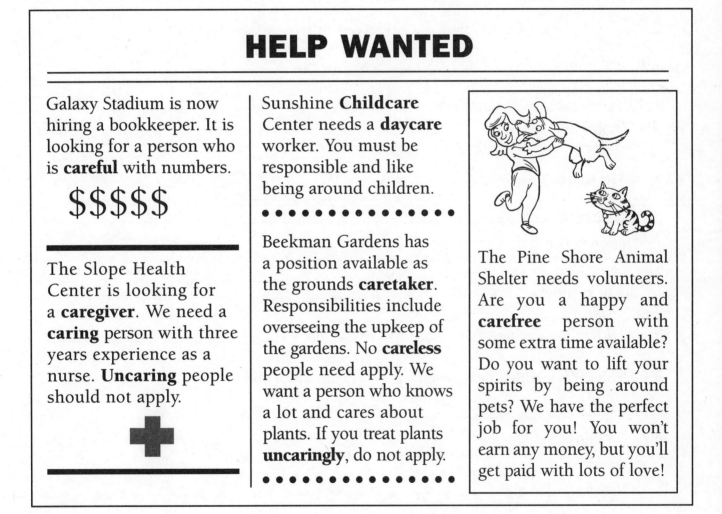

HELP WANTED

Galaxy Stadium is now hiring a bookkeeper. It is looking for a person who is **careful** with numbers.

$$$$$

The Slope Health Center is looking for a **caregiver**. We need a **caring** person with three years experience as a nurse. **Uncaring** people should not apply.

Sunshine **Childcare** Center needs a **daycare** worker. You must be responsible and like being around children.

Beekman Gardens has a position available as the grounds **caretaker**. Responsibilities include overseeing the upkeep of the gardens. No **careless** people need apply. We want a person who knows a lot and cares about plants. If you treat plants **uncaringly**, do not apply.

The Pine Shore Animal Shelter needs volunteers. Are you a happy and **carefree** person with some extra time available? Do you want to lift your spirits by being around pets? We have the perfect job for you! You won't earn any money, but you'll get paid with lots of love!

Kevin decided to apply for a job in **healthcare**, so he circled the ad for the Slope Health Center. He thought **carefully** about what to wear to his interview because he didn't want to dress **carelessly**. He knew that people often judge others on how neat they look.

Kevin did well in the interview. He said that people in healthcare jobs should never show **carelessness**, because they need to pay attention to every individual they are helping.

Kevin's **carefulness** made a good impression. He got the job.

Use Words in Context

carefree	carefulness	carelessly	caring	healthcare
careful	caregiver	carelessness	childcare	uncaring
carefully	careless	caretaker	daycare	uncaringly

Directions Write an answer to each question on the line. Use the word in boldface in your answer.

1. What is one responsibility that a **caregiver** for a baby might have?

_____

2. If you make a model airplane, why should you be **careful** when measuring?

_____

3. What is one thing you might see children doing at a **daycare** center?

_____

4. If you are **careless** when you put away the pieces to a jigsaw puzzle, what might happen

the next time you try to use it? _____

5. How might a **caring** person react to a crying child? _____

6. If you show **carelessness** when you pour sugar into your lemonade, what might

happen?_____

7. If you do your homework **carefully**, what effect might it have on your

grades?_____

8. If you address a letter to a friend **carelessly**, what might happen to it?

_____

- -

Write a Letter of Recommendation Select one of your favorite characters from a book you have read. Think about whether this character would make a good babysitter or not. Then write a letter of recommendation for this character. (If you think that the character does not have the qualities to be a good babysitter, tell why.) Use as many *care* words as you can.

Review and Extend

carefree	carefulness	carelessly	caring	healthcare
careful	caregiver	carelessness	childcare	uncaring
carefully	careless	caretaker	daycare	uncaringly

Directions Antonyms are words that have opposite meanings. They are also the same part of speech. First find an antonym for each boldface word. Then write the antonym pair in the sentences.

1. An antonym for **careless** is _____.

2. Jared was _____ and left his bike out in the rain. Next time,

he will be more _____ with his things.

3. An antonym for **caring** is _____.

4. Everyone thought that the man was mean and _____. It turned out

that he was shy but really kind and _____.

5. An antonym for **carefully** is _____.

6. If you treat your toys _____, they will last a long time.

If you treat them _____, they will break.

7. An antonym for **carefulness** is _____.

8. _____ is very important when you are driving.

_____ can lead to accidents.

Bonus Write your own sentence using a pair of antonyms.

_____

. . . .

Use Antonyms Choose two pairs of antonyms from the list above that were not already used in the sentences. Write them in your personal word journal. Then write two sentences, using one word in each sentence.

Check Your Mastery

Directions Choose the best word to complete each item. Write the word in the blank.

1. The Sunshine School provides _____ for young children.

caring   childcare   caretaker

2. The _____ plumber did a sloppy job fixing the sink.

careful   carelessness   careless

3. Because he was interested in helping others, he wanted a career in _____.

healthcare   carefulness   carelessness

4. The _____ gave the sick man his medicine.

daycare   caretaker   caregiver

5. Dan enjoyed the _____ time he had during spring break.

carefree   careful   uncaringly

6. Always handle a sharp knife _____.

carefully   healthcare   uncaring

7. The _____ of the museum had the roof repaired.

caregiver   daycare   caretaker

8. Be _____ when you wind the watch because it is
an antique from my great-grandfather.

carelessly   careful   uncaring

9. Gloria lost her sweater because of her _____.

carefulness   carelessly   carelessness

10. The _____ parents made sure their children
dressed warmly for the cold.

childcare   careless   caring

CHAPTER 3

Content Words

17 Words to Get You Ready for Algebra

Learn Words About a New Subject

equation	symbol
is greater than	variable
is less than	

Word Learning Tip!

When you read about a new subject in mathematics, such as algebra, you may see content words you don't know. These words are not the words that you read in most other books. They may also be the longest and most difficult words in the text. A clue to their meaning is that content words tell about the main topic. In this lesson, all the context words tell about algebra. Even if you don't know their meaning, you know that they are connected to the idea of algebra.

Vocabulary Building Strategy

When you read a new content word, you can learn its meaning by thinking about how it relates to the big idea in the text you are reading. Use this big idea to determine the exact meaning of each content word.

Directions As you look at the pictures and read the speech balloons, think about how the boldface words are connected to the topic. They work together to give you a big picture of algebra.

An **equation** is a number sentence that shows two equal amounts. I can simplify this equation to find out if both sides are equal. I add 5 + 3 and 6 + 2 to get 8 each time. Both sides of the equation are equal.

$5 + 3 = 6 + 2$

Here's another equation. I know what each **symbol** means: + means "plus," − means "minus," and = means "is equal to." I know that both sides of the equation have to be equal. So, I add 2 + 2 and get 4. Then I simplify 5 − 1 to get 4. Both sides of the equation are equal.

$2 + 2 = 5 - 1$

Learn Words About a New Subject

This equation has two unknown numbers in it. The letter *x* stands for one number and the letter *y* stands for the other. Each of these letters is called a **variable**. A *variable* is a letter that stands for a number or a set of numbers. In this equation, *x* could be 6 and *y* could be 2. Or, *x* could be 1 and *y* could be 7. Can you think of other possibilities?

$$x + y = 8$$

I use the symbol > to show when the number on the left **is greater than** the number on the right in a number sentence. The equation says that 80 *is greater than* 79.

$$80 > 79$$

I use the symbol < to show when the number on the left **is less than** the number on the right in a number sentence. The equation says that 79 *is less than* 80.

$$79 < 80$$

Connect Words and Meanings

| equation | is greater than | is less than | symbol | variable |

Directions Read each definition clue below. Then choose the vocabulary word that best fits in the blank.

1. Definition: a letter used to represent any one of a set of numbers

In $5 + y = 12$, y is a(n) _____.

2. Definition: a sign or mark that stands for something else

In $15 + 17 = 32$, + is a(n) _____ that tells you to add.

3. Definition: a mathematical statement that one set of numbers or values is equal to another set of numbers or values

There are two unknown quantities in the _____ $x + y = 105$.

4. Definition: is more than or a larger number than; usually represented by the symbol >

$x > y$ means that x _____ y.

5. Definition: is not as much as or has fewer than; usually represented by the symbol <

$x < y$ means that x _____ y.

Directions Complete each sentence below. Write your answer in the blank.

6. A **symbol** is a _____ that stands for something else.

7. An **equation** shows two _____ amounts.

8. A number that **is greater than** another number can be shown using the symbol

_____.

9. A **variable** is a _____ that stands for any one of a set of numbers.

10. A number that **is less than** another number can be shown using the symbol

_____.

⭐ **Understand How Content Words Are Connected** *Algebra* comes from an Arabic word meaning "solution." The ancient Egyptians and Babylonians were the first to use algebra to solve problems. *Symbol* comes from a Greek word meaning "sign." In your personal word journal, tell either how *algebra* is connected to *solution* or how *symbol* is connected to *sign*.

Use Content Words

| equation | is greater than | is less than | symbol | variable |

Directions Here is a list of facts about algebra. You might find these facts listed in a mathematics book. Write a vocabulary word in each blank to complete the sentence.

Fact 1: Here is a number sentence. 37 < 45. This means that 37 _____45.

Fact 2: In algebra, a(n) _____ is a number sentence that shows two equal amounts.

Fact 3: The _____ for *is greater than* is >.

Fact 4: A _____ is a letter that stands for a number.

You can use *x*, *y*, or *n* to stand for this number.

Fact 5: Here is a number sentence. 52 > 30. This means that 52 _____ 30.

Directions Notice the vocabulary word in each Fact statement. Write a word in each blank that shows that you understand the vocabulary word.

Fact 6: An **equation** is a mathematical sentence about two _____ sets of numbers.

Fact 7: A **variable** is a letter that stands for one or more _____

numbers. For example, if Josie and Josh have 5 coins, you know that x + y = 5.

Fact 8: A **symbol** or sign can tell you to do one of these operations: add, subtract, multiply, or

_____.

Fact 9: The symbol _____ between numbers means

that the number on the left is greater than the number on the right.

Fact 10: The symbol _____ between numbers means

that the number on the left is less than the number on the right.

· ·

★ **Create Equations** Write five algebra equations on one sheet of paper and their answers on a different sheet of paper. Give your equations to another student. Ask this student to write the content words below the symbols you used in your problems, and then solve the problems. After completing these two steps, check the answers. Make a list of any new content words you use.

17 Words to Get You Ready for Algebra

Put Words Into Action

| equation | is greater than | is less than | symbol | variable |

Directions Read the passage below. Select the vocabulary word that best fits the context. Write the word in the blank.

> Here is a problem. There are 8 pets at Annie's house. Some are cats and some are dogs. There are more cats than dogs. How many are there of each? Write all the possible answers.

First, use letters to stand for the unknown numbers of dogs and cats. Since these numbers will vary, we can call the letter that stands for them a (**1**)_____ (*symbol, variable, equation*). Use x to stand for the number of cats. Use y to stand for the number of dogs. Then write this (**2**)_____ (*symbol, variable, equation*): $x + y = 8$. The (**3**) _____ (*symbol, variable, equation*) + tells you that you will be adding x and y. You know that x must be a number that (**4**) _____ (*is greater than, is less than*) y, because there are more cats than dogs. You know that y must be a number that (**5**) _____ (*is greater than, is less than*) x, because there are fewer dogs than cats.

Here are all the possible answers to this problem.

x = cats	y = dogs
5	3
6	2
7	1

BONUS

6. Write an equation to find out the value of y if $x = 5$. _____

7. Write an equation to find out the value of x if $y = 1$. _____

8. Write the answer to each equation. _____

_____

Write a Word Problem Use the problem above as a model. Write a word problem for your partner to solve. Then exchange papers with your partner. Write an equation to solve your partner's problem. Record any new content words you use.

Review and Extend

equation	is greater than	is less than	symbol	variable

BONUS WORDS Here are four new words that relate to algebra. Remember that these words all deal with the same big idea as your vocabulary words. That means that even if you have never seen these words before, you do know one important fact—they all tell you something about this form of mathematics called algebra.

set A set is a group of numbers. This is a set of numbers: 2, 4, 6, 8, 10.
subset A subset is part of a set. A subset is made up of some of the numbers in the set. 2, 4, 6 are a subset of the set 2, 4, 6, 8, 10.
formula A formula is a rule that is expressed by using variables and numbers.
factor A factor is one of two or more numbers that are multiplied to make a product. In this number sentence, $6 \times 5 = 30$, 6 and 5 are factors of 30.

Directions Read each item below. Choose the vocabulary word or the new content word that best fits the context. Write the word in the blank.

1. This group of numbers—6, 8, 10, 12, 14—is called a _____ of numbers.

2. Here is a set of numbers: 1, 3, 5, 7, 9. The numbers 3, 5, 7 are a _____ of this larger set.

3. Tomas wants to find out how much wood he needs to build a doghouse. He makes up a way to solve his problem. He uses this _____: *height* times *width* times *depth*. It is written like this: $D = hwd$.

4. Kareem has 20 dollars to spend on music CDs. He needs to know the 2 or more numbers that can be multiplied to make 20. Another name for the numbers to be multiplied is _____(s).

5. Denise had to solve this _____: $y - 15 = 20$. The letter y is called a _____. The minus sign is called a _____.

⭐ **Write About Algebra** Algebra is used every day by scientists and mathematicians. With a partner, talk about how algebra might help you solve a problem. Then write about one situation in which you could use algebra to solve a problem. Use at least two vocabulary words and three new content words you have learned this week by using the Word Learning Tip and Vocabulary Building Strategy.

17 **Words to Get You Ready for Algebra**

Check Your Mastery

Directions Read each item below. Circle the vocabulary word that best fits in each sentence.

1. A(n) _____ stands for an unknown number or set of numbers.

   A. variable   **B.** symbol   **C.** equation

2. A(n) _____ might look like this: x + y = 20.

   A. symbol   **B.** variable   **C.** equation

3. The _____ x means "to multiply."

   A. equation   **B.** symbol   **C.** variable

4. If *n* < 40, you know that *n* is a number that _____ 40.

   A. is greater than   **B.** is less than   **C.** is equal to

5. If *n* > 40, you know that *n* is a number that _____ 40.

   A. is greater than   **B.** is less than   **C.** is equal to

Directions Look at the item below. Then write a vocabulary word in the blank in each sentence.

$$x + 12 > y + 5$$
$$x + y = 30$$

This is a very difficult (**6**)_____, thought Kevin.

The first (**7**)_____ is represented by the letter *x*.

The (**8**)_____ > tells me that the first set of numbers

(**9**)_____ the second set of numbers. If the > symbol were

turned in the other direction it would mean (**10**)_____.

Learn Words About a New Subject

Directions The panels below are a storyboard for a video. Look at the pictures and the dialogue. Think about how the boldface words are connected to the big idea of how living things depend on each other for food..

We're going to see how living things depend on one another for food. That's called a **food chain.**

That means one animal eats another, right?

FOOD CHAINS

Cool!

This is the beginning of the ocean **food chain.** The small plants floating in the ocean are called algae. They make their food from sunlight. The krill are like shrimp. They eat algae. Krill are **herbivores**, which means they eat only plants.

COD FISH

KRILL

ALGAE

KRILL

I'm definitely not a **herbivore**!

Vocabulary Words

carnivore   omnivore

food chain   prey

herbivore

Word Learning Tip!

When you read about a new subject, you may see new content words that you haven't seen in everyday reading. These words are often the longest and most difficult words in the text. They tell something specific about the topic. To learn these new words, think about the big idea or subject about which you are reading. All of the words in this lesson tell how living things depend on one another for food. They all tell about how animals eat.

Vocabulary Building Strategy

To learn the meaning of content words that tell about a new subject, make connections between the unknown words and the big idea or subject you are reading about. Tie together the big idea and the meanings of other content words you know in the text. This will help you learn the meaning of unknown words.

18 Words About How Living Things Depend on One Another

Learn Words About a New Subject

| carnivore | food chain | herbivore | omnivore | prey |

FOOD CHAIN

WHALE

SEAL

SEAL

COD FISH

Here is the rest of the ocean **food chain**. These animals are all **carnivores**. They eat only meat. The cod eats the krill. The seal eats the cod, and the whale eats the seal. The animal that is hunted and eaten is called the **prey**.

Humans eat animals, like your tuna fish sandwich. We also eat plants, like that salad. We are **omnivores**.

We eat everything! We are **omnivores**!

Connect Words and Meanings

> | carnivore | food chain | herbivore | omnivore | prey |

Directions Write the vocabulary word that best fits each definition. You may use your dictionary or the glossary to help you.

1. **Definition:** a living creature that eats a wide variety of plants and animals _____

2. **Definition:** a living creature that eats only or mostly plants _____

3. **Definition:** a living creature that is only or mostly a meat eater _____

4. **Definition:** a chain of living beings in which smaller and weaker creatures are eaten by larger and stronger creatures _____

5. **Definition:** an animal that is hunted and eaten by another animal (or even by a meat-eating plant!) _____

Directions Write the vocabulary word that best fits in each blank. Use each vocabulary word only once.

A (**6**)_____ is made up of living creatures that eat one another. One example can be seen in the grasslands of Africa. An antelope is a (**7**)_____ that feeds on the grass. The lion is a (**8**)_____ that eats only meat. The lion hunts and then eats the antelope, which is its (**9**)_____. Monkeys live in the rain forests of Africa. They eat plant leaves and fruits. Monkeys also eat birds, birds' eggs, insects, and lizards. A monkey is an (**10**) _____.

★ **Make Connections Among Words** Many science words contain Latin roots. The three words that describe "eaters" in a food chain are *carnivore*, *herbivore*, and *omnivore*. The root *–vore* comes from the Latin word *vorore*, which means "to eat up completely." Other Latin roots are *carni–*, which means "meat," *herba–* which means "a plant with seeds," and *omni–*, which means "all." In your personal word journal, tell how these roots make up the meaning of these three words: *carnivore*, *herbivore*, and *omnivore*.

18 Words About How Living Things Depend on One Another

Use Content Words

| carnivore | food chain | herbivore | omnivore | prey |

Directions Look at the food chains below. The first item that is eaten is at the bottom of the food chain. Write the vocabulary word that fits best in each sentence.

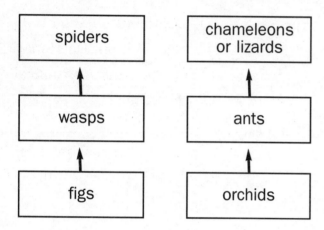

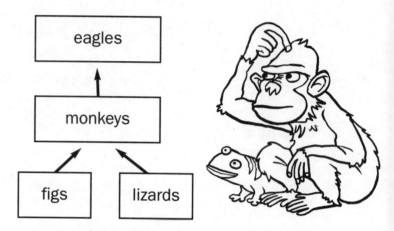

1. A food web shows the different food chains in an environment. Figs, wasps, and spiders make up one

   _____

   in the rain-forest food web.

2. The wasp is the _____ of the spider that eats it.

3. The eagle is a(n) _____ that eats meat.

4. An ant is a(n) _____ because it eats only plants, such as orchids and other flowers.

5. An adult wasp feeds mainly on fruit and sugar. It eats figs. Is the wasp a carnivore or an herbivore? _____

6. The monkey is a(n)

   _____

   because it eats both figs and lizards.

7. An animal can be the

   _____

   of a stronger, larger, or fiercer animal.

8. A chameleon eats mostly ants and other insects. Is the chameleon a carnivore or an herbivore? _____

9. One _____

   in the rain forest begins with orchids.

10. A spider traps wasps and other insects in its web and then eats them. Is the spider a carnivore or an herbivore?

    _____

Create a Food Chain Put a plant at the bottom of a food chain and show the animal or animals that eat it. Next, add an animal that eats the plant-eating animal. Look in an encyclopedia for information. Label each animal with the word *carnivore*, *herbivore*, or *omnivore*.

Words About How Living Things Depend on One Another **18**

Put Words Into Action

carnivore	food chain	herbivore	omnivore	prey

Directions Read the animal riddles below. Answer each riddle question with a vocabulary word. Write it in the blank.

1. I am a rabbit. My fear is that an owl, hawk, or coyote will catch and eat me. What is the word that describes an animal like me that is hunted by other animals?

_____

2. I am a horse that eats hay. I like oats and apples, too. I do not eat meat. What is the name for an animal like me?

_____

3. I am a bear that eats mice, squirrels, and fish. Birds' eggs and worms are my favorite snacks. But I'm also famous for eating honey. I like berries, fruits, nuts, and the leaves and roots of plants. I guess you could say I'm an all-around eater. What is the name for an animal like me?

_____

4. I'm a tiger. We are strict meat eaters. What is the name for an animal like me?

_____

5. In a forest, squirrels eat seeds and nuts. A fox mother kills a squirrel for food for her babies, which are called kits. Later, a hawk steals a kit for its dinner. What is the name for this way of nature?

_____

6. The bald eagle is the national bird of the United States. This bird eats small animals. What is the name of an animal with these eating habits?

_____

7. What is a word for the small animals, such as squirrels, rabbits, and birds, that an eagle hunts?

_____

8. Sheep, goats, and camels eat grass. What is the vocabulary word that describes all these animals?

_____

9. Last night, I ate chicken, rice, and carrots. What word describes my eating habits?

_____

10. Alligators eat water snakes that eat fish that eat worms that eat water plants. What is the way these living things are linked together called?

_____

Create a Collage Cut pictures from magazines and put them in food chains. Label the pictures using vocabulary words and write a caption that describes the big idea to which all of your content words connect.

18 Words About How Living Things Depend on One Another

Review and Extend

carnivore	food chain	herbivore	omnivore	prey

BONUS WORDS Here are two new words about food chains. Remember that these words all deal with the same big idea as your vocabulary words. That means that even if you have never seen these words before, you do know one important thing— they both tell you something about how living creatures depend on one another for food.

predator an animal that lives by hunting other animals for food

Example: a shark

ecosystem a community of plants and animals that is affected by its environment, including the air, water, sunlight, and soil

Example: all the plants and animals in a lake

Directions Read each item below. Choose the vocabulary word or the new content word that best fits the context. Write it in the blank.

All the plants and animals that live in a forest form a(n) (**1**) _____.

The plants use sunlight, soil, and water to make their own food. Plant-eating birds and

animals are called (**2**)_____. They eat grass, seeds, nuts, roots, and leaves.

Larger and stronger animals often hunt these plant eaters. These (**3**)_____(s),

or hunters, depend on the animals that are their (**4**)_____. Without

them, the meat eaters, or (**5**) _____, would go hungry.

If there is a change in an (**6**) _____, all the members of the

community are affected. If there is too little rain, some plants may die. Some of the animals

that eat these plants will die also. Without (**7**)_____ to hunt,

the (**8**)_____ will have to move elsewhere to find meat. They will

need to join a new community or they will die.

⭐ **Think About It** Think about the teeth of lions and tigers. Why do you think that carnivores such as these need long, sharp teeth? Write in your personal word journal to explain your answer. Use as many vocabulary words as you can and other content words that connect to the big idea of how lions and tigers eat.

Check Your Mastery

Directions Read each question below. Circle the letter of the choice that best answers each question.

1. Which vocabulary word best describes the eating habits of a cat that feeds on mice?
   A. herbivore   **B.** prey   **C.** carnivore

2. Which vocabulary word explains that humans eat a variety of plants and animals?
   A. omnivore   **B.** carnivore   **C.** herbivore

3. What do you call an animal that is hunted by another animal?
   A. food chain   **B.** prey   **C.** carnivore

4. The Venus flytrap is a plant that eats insects. Which word describes this plant's eating habits?
   A. herbivore   **B.** carnivore   **C.** prey

5. A flower makes a sweet juice called nectar. A hummingbird drinks the nectar. Which word describes the bird's eating habits?
   A. herbivore   **B.** carnivore   **C.** omnivore

6. A shrimp eats plants in the ocean. A fish eats the shrimp. Then a seal eats the fish. Finally, a polar bear kills the seal and eats it. What do you call this feeding sequence?
   A. carnivore   **B.** omnivore   **C.** food chain

7. An owl hunts for a mouse. The owl is called the predator. What do you call the mouse?
   A. prey   **B.** carnivore   **C.** food chain

8. Which word describes how sheep, goats, cows, and deer, which eat mostly grass and other plants, eat?
   A. food chain   **B.** omnivore   **C.** herbivore

9. A lizard in the desert eats insects. Then a snake eats the lizard. A coyote later kills and eats the snake. What name describes what occurs among this set of animals?
   A. herbivore   **B.** food chain   **C.** prey

10. A monkey in the rain forest will eat figs and bananas. It will also eat meat when it can. Which vocabulary word describes its eating habits?
   A. carnivore   **B.** herbivore   **C.** omnivore

19 Words About Volcanoes

Learn Words About a New Subject

Vocabulary Words

crater	lava
dormant	magma
eruption	

Word Learning Tip!

When you read words about a new subject, you may see words that you have not seen before in your everyday reading. These words are often the longest and most difficult words in the text. They tell you something specific about the topic. To learn these new words, think about the big idea or subject. In this lesson, all of the words tell about volcanoes.

Vocabulary Building Strategy

To learn the meaning of content words that tell about a new subject, make connections between the unknown word and the big idea or subject. The new word will tell something specific about that big idea or subject. Tie together the big idea and the meanings of other content words that you know in the text. This will help you learn the exact meaning of the unknown content words.

Directions Look at the diagram of a volcano erupting, or exploding. Read the text and labels to learn about the parts of a volcano and about how the explosion of a volcano happens.

Eruption of a Volcano

The **eruption** of a volcano is a terrifying sight. A volcano can be **dormant**, or "sleeping," for a long time. Then it can explode or erupt. Melted rock called **magma** pushes through the mountain and comes out of the **crater**. The **magma** becomes **lava**, or hot liquid, that flows down the mountain. Hot ash and gases also come out of the crater. This is called an **eruption**.

Lava is hot liquid rock that pours out of a volcano when it erupts. Hot ashes mix with lava as it flows down the mountain. When the lava and ash cool, they form new rock on the mountain.

A **dormant** volcano is one that is not active. But it could erupt again and then the volcano is active, not **dormant**.

The mouth of the volcano is called the **crater**. Melted rock, gases, ashes, and pieces of rock come out of this opening.

A **vent** is the tunnel through which melted rock moves up to the **crater**.

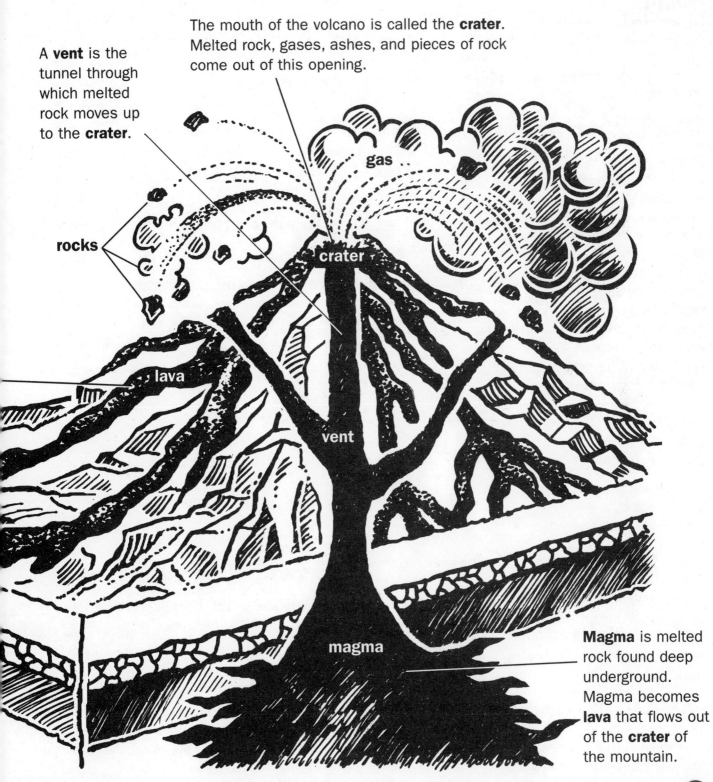

rocks

gas

crater

lava

vent

magma

Magma is melted rock found deep underground. Magma becomes **lava** that flows out of the **crater** of the mountain.

Connect Words and Meanings

| crater | dormant | eruption | lava | magma |

Directions First choose the vocabulary word that matches each definition. Then fill in the blank in the sentence that follows the definition. You may use a dictionary or the glossary to help you.

1. **Definition:** the hot liquid that flows out of a volcano _____

2. The _____ flowed down the mountain like syrup.

3. **Definition:** sleeping or not active _____

4. Most of the time, volcanoes are _____. They may not erupt for hundreds of years.

5. **Definition:** the mouth of a volcano; the cup-shaped hole or cavity at the top of

   the volcano _____

6. When the volcano erupted, hot gas, rocks, and lava came bursting out of the
   _____ of the mountain.

7. **Definition:** the melted rock deep beneath Earth's surface _____

8. The _____ pushed its way through the mountain and created an explosion.

9. **Definition:** the name for a volcano exploding _____

10. The _____ of a volcano is often a terrible disaster. People can be hurt or
    killed and property can be destroyed.

⭐ **Find Out More About Volcanoes** Use the library, your textbook, or the Internet to find out more about volcanoes. Record three interesting facts. Then find three new content words about volcanoes and write them in your personal word journal. Tell how you used the Word Learning Tip and Vocabulary Building Strategy to learn their meaning.

Use Content Words

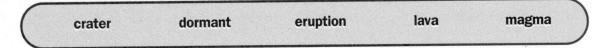

| crater | dormant | eruption | lava | magma |

Directions Below are interesting facts about the volcanoes. Fill in the blanks in the sentences with the vocabulary word that fits best.

1. Volcanoes form wherever there is hot, melted rock called _____ under the ground. This hot rock pushes through the cooler rock until an explosion occurs.

2. Mount Vesuvius erupted in ancient Roman times. The _____ that flowed out of the mountain poured into the Roman town of Herculaneum. It filled the town and the harbor.

3. The Roman town of Pompeii was buried under ash and pieces of rock. Ashes and rock blasted out of the _____ at the top of Vesuvius. Pompeii was dug out in the 1700s. People now visit the town to see what Roman life was like thousands of years ago.

4. Mauna Loa is the world's largest volcano. It erupted about 50 years ago. Since then, it has been _____.

5. The _____ of Mont Pelee destroyed the city of Saint Pierre. Thirty-eight thousand people were killed by the poisonous gases from the volcano.

6. Some volcanoes are under the ocean floor. When the volcano erupts, it makes a _____ or opening in the ocean floor.

7. A volcano called Stromboli is in the Mediterranean Sea near Italy. The

_____

of Stromboli seldom stops. The volcano can be erupting for months or even years at a time.

8. _____ from underwater volcanoes collects on the ocean floor and makes underwater mountains.

9. In 1982, El Chichon in Mexico erupted and killed 187 people. It is now "sleeping," or

_____.

10. The _____ of Krakatoa produced waves in the ocean that were 130 feet high. The waves drowned 36,000 people who lived on islands near the blast.

. . . .

⭐ **Understand Words Related to Science** The word *volcano* comes from Vulcan, the Roman name for their god of fire. Romans believed that Vulcan lived in the sea under an island. They called this island Vulcano. The island was created by lava from an underwater volcano. Use your dictionary or the Internet to find three other words that come from Greek and Roman myths that are related to science.

19 Words About Volcanoes

Put Words Into Action

crater	dormant	eruption	lava	magma

Directions Read the paragraphs. Fill in the blanks with the vocabulary word that fits best.

The Eruption of Mount St. Helens

Mount St. Helens is a volcano in Washington state. It had been (**1**) _____ for close to 100 years. Then on May 18, 1980, Mt. St. Helens erupted. Steam and ash were blown out of the side of the mountain. This made a(n) (**2**) _____ or opening on the side, not the top, of the mountain. That was unusual because a crater is usually at the top of a mountain.

The people in nearby towns were surprised by the (**3**) _____ of Mt. St. Helens. But scientists knew the volcano would erupt sooner or later. Under Mt. St. Helens, there was melted rock called (**4**) _____. The last explosion had created a long vent or tunnel inside the mountain. The gases from the magma pushed it up through the vent. The gases made a hole called a(n) (**5**) _____ in the side of the mountain. A blast sent rocks, ash, and gases out of the mountain. A liquid, made of melted rocks, called (**6**) _____, came flowing out of the hole also. Later, when the (**7**) _____ began to cool, it hardened into rock.

Mt. St. Helens is once more a (**8**) _____, or "sleeping," volcano. But it could erupt again. There is still (**9**) _____, or hot, melted rock, under the ground. It could push its way through the mountain once again. This would cause another (**10**) _____ of Mt. St. Helens.

. . . .

⭐ **Write an Eyewitness Report** Imagine that you lived in a town near Mount St. Helens. Use the information in the passage above to write about what you saw and heard as the volcano exploded. Be sure to tell how you felt as the eruption was happening. Use as many of the vocabulary words as you can.

Review and Extend

| crater | dormant | eruption | lava | magma |

BONUS WORDS Here are two new words that describe volcanoes. Remember that these words all deal with the same big idea as your vocabulary words. That means that even if you have never seen these words before, you know that they have to do with volcanoes. You can use what you already know about volcanoes to understand the meanings of these words.

extinct used to describe a volcano that has burned itself out and will probably not erupt in the future

inactive used to describe a volcano that is dormant, but could erupt in the future

Directions The paragraphs below are part of a travel brochure. They tell about various trips tourists can take to see volcanoes around the world. Read each trip description and fill in the vocabulary or bonus word that best fits in each blank.

VISIT THE WORLD'S GREAT VOLCANOES

Trip # 1 Mount Fuji is the highest mountain in Japan. It was once an active, or erupting, volcano. Now, it is a(n)
1. _____,
or dormant, volcano. Thousands of people climb to the top to see the mountain's
2. _____, or opening. Because the volcano is not active, it is safe to be there.

Trip # 2 Aconcagua is a mountain in Argentina. It was once a volcano, but it is now
3. _____.
It has burnt itself out. The whole upper part of the mountain has crumbled away.

Trip # 3 Would you like to see a volcano that is always erupting? Then visit a volcano named Stromboli. You can see and hear its many _____(s).
4. _____ The reason it is always erupting is that
5. _____ inside the volcano is producing gas. The escaping gas causes a lot of explosions. Come see it on an island off the coast of Italy.

⭐ **Learn New Words About Travel** Pick a place you would like to travel to. Gather information about it from books, the Internet, and travel brochures. Identify at least three new words about travel. Write them in your journal and tell how the Word Learning Tip and Vocabulary Building Strategy helped you to learn their meaning.

Check Your Mastery

Directions Match the words on the left with the correct definition on the right. Write the letter of the definition in the blank by the vocabulary word.

___ **1.** crater   **A.** the explosion of a volcano

___ **2.** lava   **B.** a word that describes an inactive volcano

___ **3.** eruption   **C.** melted rocks that push up from under the ground

___ **4.** magma   **D.** the hot liquid that flows out of a volcano

___ **5.** dormant   **E.** the bowl-shaped opening created by a volcano exploding

Directions Read the multiple-choice questions below. Circle the letter in front of the correct answer.

6. What is the difference between **magma** and **lava**?

    A. None, they are the same thing.

    B. Magma is under the ground and lava comes out of the volcano.

    C. Lava is under the ground and magma comes out of the volcano.

7. What might you see at the **dormant** volcano?

    A. tourists exploring the crater

    B. gas and rocks exploding out of the mountain

    C. lava flowing down the mountain

8. Where might you see the **crater** of a volcano?

    A. inside the mountain

    B. underground

    C. at the top of the mountain

9. Which of these things does NOT happen during the **eruption** of a volcano?

    A. Lava, rocks, and ash are blown out of the mountain.

    B. There is always peace and quiet.

    C. There is an explosion, like a bottle blowing its top.

10. What might you see flowing down the side of a mountain?

    A. crater

    B. lava

    C. dormant

Learn Words About a New Subject

Vocabulary Words

ballot	political party
candidate	register
election	

Word Learning Tip!

When you read about a new subject, you see many content words you have never seen before. They are often the longest words and describe difficult concepts about the subject. They are not words you read in a lot of other books. To learn them, think about the big idea that you are reading about and what part of it the new word is describing.

Vocabulary Building Strategy

When you read new context words, you can make associations and connections between that word and the subject and other long context words. You know that all the context words tell something important about the topic. You can use the subject, or big idea, and the setting that the author described so far in the text to determine the exact meaning of each context word.

Learn Words About a New Subject

ballot   candidate   election   political party   register

Connect Words and Meanings

| ballot | candidate | election | political party | register |

Directions Read each definition below. Then complete the sentence that follows it.

1. register: to enter your name formally so that you can vote

If you don't **register** to vote, _____.

2. ballot: a secret way of voting, or a sheet of paper or a card used so a vote can be counted

Mark the **ballot** carefully so that _____.

3. election: the act or process of choosing someone or deciding something by voting

It is important to hold an **election** because _____.

4. political party: an organized group of people with similar beliefs who try to win elections

A **political party** might celebrate when _____.

5. candidate: someone who is running for an office in an election

I would vote for one **candidate** over another if _____.

Directions Read each sentence below, paying special attention to the boldface clue. In the blank, write the vocabulary word that can be used to replace these words.

6. The town was holding an (**activity in which you choose a person**) _____ for mayor.

7. One (**person running for office**) _____ made a speech at the shopping center.

8. "Remember my name," he said, "when you fill out your (**sheet of paper used for voting**) _____."

9. "And don't forget to (**enter your name formally so that you can vote**) _____," he said.

10. Then people passed out shopping bags with the candidate's name and the name of his (**organized group of people with similar beliefs**) _____.

⭐ **Understand Words About Voting** In ancient Rome, a candidate for office wore a white robe to show that he was pure. The white robe showed that no one controlled the candidate or could tell that candidate what to do. The Latin word for white is *candidus*, and it is from this word that we get our word *candidate*. In your personal word journal, tell what qualities you think a candidate for office should have. Use at least two vocabulary words. Also, use two new content words you have learned this week by using the Word Learning Tip and Vocabulary Building Strategy.

20 Words About Voting

Use Content Words

> ballot   candidate   election   political party   register

Directions Use your content words to fill out the process chart below.

THE (**1**) _____ PROCESS

(**2**) _____ to vote.

↓

Learn about the people each (**3**) _____ recommends.

↓

Listen to the (**4**) _____ (s) as they debate the issues.

↓

Decide which (**5**) _____ you think is the best for the job.

↓

Mark the day of the (**6**) _____ on your calendar.

↓

Fill out a(n) (**7**) _____ for the candidate of your choice.

↓

Make sure you mark your (**8**) _____ correctly.

⭐ **Write About Voting** Voting in elections is very important for our system of government to work. This is how "we the people" make our voices heard. It is how we exercise our power. The number of people who register to vote and actually cast their votes should be 100 percent, but it is far from it. In your personal word journal, write three or four reasons why you think it is important to vote. Use at lease three vocabulary words in your sentences.

Put Words Into Action

> ballot   candidate   election   political party   register

Directions Imagine you are a reporter covering an election. You want to make sure that you have mastered the words you need to write about this topic. Read each situation in the left-hand column. Then write the content word you would use in the right-hand column. Also, write a sentence using the word.

Situation: You want to report on the voting record of one of the people who is running. What word would you use for this person?

1. Word _____
2. Sentence _____
_____

Situation: You want to report about the event that happened four years ago in which people voted. What word would you use to describe the event?

3. Word _____
4. Sentence _____
_____

Situation: You want to compare the groups that are supporting each person who is running. What word would you use to name such a group?

5. Word _____
6. Sentence _____
_____

Situation: You want to report the secret way in which people vote. What word would you use to tell what people used to mark their votes?

7. Word _____
8. Sentence _____
_____

Situation: You want to report the reason some people were unable to vote. What word would you use to tell what they did not do?

9. Word _____
10. Sentence _____
_____

⭐ **Write a Speech** Imagine your school is holding an election for class president. Write a speech telling why you or some other candidate should be elected. (The candidate does not have to be a real person.) Use at least three vocabulary words in your speech and two new content words that you have learned this week using the Word Learning Tip and Vocabulary Building Strategy.

Review and Extend

| ballot | candidate | election | political party | register |

BONUS WORDS Here are three new words about voting. Remember that these words all deal with the same big idea as your vocabulary words. That means that even if you have never seen these words before, you do know one important fact—they all tell you something about voting.

endorse to support or approve someone or something

poll a survey of people's opinions and beliefs

polls the place where votes are cast and recorded during an election

Directions Read each item below. Choose the vocabulary word or the new bonus word that best fits the context. Write it in the blank.

Make sure you cast your vote for the (**1**)_____ of your

choice before the (**2**)_____ close at 10 P.M.

The homeowners group decided to (**3**)_____ Miguel Rodriguez

instead of the person recommended by the other (**4**)_____.

According to the latest (**5**) _____, if the election were

held today, Sonia Jamison would win.

Remember to (**6**)_____ so that you can vote

during the (**7**)_____.

Look at the (**8**)_____ carefully before you fill it out

so that you don't mark a vote for the wrong (**9**)_____.

A (**10**)_____ shows how voters feel about different issues.

⭐ **Search for More Words About Voting** Look through newspapers or newsmagazines or listen to a newscast on television. In your personal word journal, record three new words you learned about voting using the Word Learning Tip and Vocabulary Building Strategy. Write what each one means.

Check Your Mastery

Directions Read each item below. Write the vocabulary word that best fits in each sentence.

1. Some states use a paper _____, while others use a voting machine.

    A. ballot   **B.** candidate   **C.** election

2. The symbol of one _____ is a donkey, and of the other is an elephant.

    A. political party   **B.** register   **C.** ballot

3. Before you can vote, you have to _____.

    A. ballot   **B.** election   **C.** register

4. Ravi Stantos is the _____ I will select.

    A. political party   **B.** candidate   **C.** ballot

5. You have to be eighteen years old to vote in a presidential _____.

    A. candidate   **B.** election   **C.** register

Directions Read the passage below. Select the vocabulary word that best fits the context. Write it in the blank.

There is a(n) (**6**) _____ (*election, register, ballot*) for President every four

years on the first Tuesday after the first Monday in November.

Each (**7**)_____ (*candidate, political party, ballot*) creates a list of

(**8**) _____s (*election, register, candidate*) this group wants you to vote for.

The names of the people running for office appear on the (**9**)_____

(*ballot, political party, candidate*). But you can't vote for them unless you are

(**10**) _____(ed) (*register, candidate, election*).

Learn Words About a New Subject

Vocabulary Words

figure of speech
literal
metaphor
personification
simile

Word Learning Tip!

When you read about a new subject, you may see words you have not seen before in your everyday reading. These words are often the longest and most difficult in the text. They tell you something specific about the subject. To learn these new words, think about the big idea or subject about which you are reading. In this lesson, all content words deal with figurative language, a special way to use words.

Vocabulary Building Strategy

To learn the meaning of content words that tell about a new subject, make connections between the unknown word and the big idea or subject. The new word will tell something specific about that big idea or subject. Tie together the big idea and the meanings of other content words that you know in the text. This will help you determine the exact meaning of the unknown content words.

Directions As you look at the pictures below and on page 153, think about how the boldface words are connected to the topic of figurative language. Use the examples and the words below them to learn the exact meaning of each vocabulary word.

When I'm feeling lonely, I listen to my music.

This is a **literal** statement. It means just what the words say.

Music is good company!

This is a **figure of speech**. It says the same thing as the **literal** statement. But it says it in a poetic or imaginative way by putting two words together that don't usually connect to the same big idea, like *music* and *company*.

A **simile** is one kind of **figure of speech**. It compares two very different content words by saying one word is like another. "Music is like a friend" is a **simile**. A **simile** uses the word *as* or *like* to make this comparison between two words.

A **metaphor** is another kind of **figure of speech**. It compares two very different words by saying that one *is* another. "Music is my best friend" is a **metaphor**. The words are not **literal**. They do not mean exactly what they say. Instead, they create an imaginative picture that shows an emotion, thought, or thing. This metaphor shows how much the boy enjoys music.

In this scene, a musical note acts like a person. It walks into a room and talks. Making a thing, idea, or word into a person is called **personification**. It's another kind of **figure of speech**.

Connect Words and Meanings

| figure of speech | literal | metaphor | personification | simile |

Directions Read each definition and example below. Then complete the sentence that follows.

1. **figure of speech** (noun): an expression in which words are used in a poetic way
   Example: He is as strong as an ox.
   Sentence: The **figure of speech** "as strong as an ox" means _____.

2. **literal** (adjective): meaning exactly what the words say
   Example: He is a very strong man.
   Sentence: It is important to write the **literal** truth when _____.

3. **simile** (noun): a figure of speech that uses the word *like* or *as* in which two very different things are said to be similar
   Example: Her eyes are as blue as the sky.
   Sentence: "The baby is as sweet as sugar" is a **simile** because _____.

4. **metaphor** (noun): a figure of speech in which one thing is said to be another thing
   Example: My love is a rose.
   Sentence: A **metaphor** is different from a simile because _____.

5. **personification** (noun): a figure of speech in which a nonliving thing acts like a human being
   Example: The soft breeze ran its fingers through the leaves of the tree.
   Sentence: The breeze is acting like a **person** because _____.

Directions Write *literal* or *figure of speech* next to each statement below.

6. My love is as deep as the sea. _____

7. The depth of the water is 36 feet. _____

8. The sun took pity on the old man and warmed him with her rays. _____

9. A book is food for the mind. _____

10. The book costs $21 _____

★ **Search for Figures of Speech** Look in a book of poems. Find an example of a simile, a metaphor, and personification. Write these figures of speech in your personal word journal and label them.

Use Content Words

| figure of speech | literal | metaphor | personification | simile |

Directions Read these instructions for how to write a poem. Fill each blank with the vocabulary word or phrase that fits best. You will use each word twice. (The plural of *figure of speech* is *figures of speech*.)

1. A poem can express your feelings or tell your thoughts about a topic. But you don't want your poem to use only _____ language, or language that means exactly what the words say. Use some figurative language, too.

2. Try to use some figures of speech. Don't just say, "I feel angry." Use a _____ such as "I could roar like a lion."

3. If you are feeling angry a lot, you might use a _____ such as " I am a lion, roaring with anger."

4. Or you could try _____. You could take a feeling and make it act like a person. For example, you could say, "Anger walked the streets of the city and made everyone afraid."

5. A poem can be like a song. It can have a regular rhythm. The lines can rhyme. These poems use word pictures called similes, metaphors, or personification. Each one is a _____.

6. Other poems can be in free verse. These poems don't rhyme. The rhythm is the same as ordinary talking. But these are still poems because they use _____ to create word pictures and express thoughts poetically.

7. A _____ uses the word *like* or *as* to show that two things are alike or similar. An example is: " I feel as swift as the wind when I run."

8. A _____ is a stronger way to say that two things are alike. An example is: "When I run, I am the wind." Can you see the difference?

9. _____ creates a word picture that can be fun to read. Take a thing or idea and make it act like a person. For example: "The clouds are weeping today."

10. Similes, metaphors, and personification are all ways for poets to express their ideas. These figures of speech are not _____ statements. They don't mean exactly what the words say. But word pictures make a poem have more meaning than just saying the literal truth. So use your imagination and see what word pictures you can create.

⭐ **Create Figures of Speech** Pick a topic you would like to write about in a poem. Write a simile, a metaphor, and a personification about that topic. Save these in your personal word journal.

Put Words Into Action

| figure of speech | literal | metaphor | personification | simile |

Directions Read each item below. Pay special attention to the vocabulary word in the instructions. Then complete the sentence. Write your answer in the blank.

1. Write a **metaphor** that expresses your feelings about a rainy day.

_____

2. Write a **simile** that shows how you feel about eating ice cream.

_____

3. Write a **figure of speech** that imaginatively tells your ideas about winning a big game.

_____

4. Use **literal** language to tell how you feel after you win a big game.

_____

5. Use **personification** to show what your refrigerator thinks every time you open the door.

_____

Directions Help Carlotta complete this composition about a poem she read. Choose the correct vocabulary word from the two in parentheses. Write the missing vocabulary word in the blank. Use each word once.

I liked the way the poet used (**6**) _____(*simile, personification*) to describe the moon. He made the moon seem so shy that she often hid her light so people couldn't find her. There was one (**7**)_____ (*metaphor, simile*) I liked a lot. It is "The light of the moon was as gentle as a cat's purr." I know these words were not meant to have their (**8**)_____ (*literal, figure of speech*), or exact, meaning, because the light of the moon and a cat's purr are two very different things. But this (**9**) _____ (*figure of speech, personification*) created an interesting word picture in my mind. Another figure of speech I liked a lot was this (**10**) _____ (*metaphor, literal*): "The moon is a silver coin tossed in the sky."

· ·

⭐ **Write Figurative and Literal Statements** Choose any two topics. Write one statement that is literal about one topic and one statement that is figurative about the other topic.

Review and Extend

| figure of speech | literal | metaphor | personification | simile |

> **BONUS WORDS** Here are two new words. Remember that these words all deal with the same big idea as your vocabulary words. That means that even if you have never seen these words before, you know that they have to do with figurative language. You can use what you already know about figurative language to understand the meanings of these words.
>
> **image** a word picture
>
> **vivid** sharp and clear

Directions Read each item below. Choose the vocabulary word or the new content word that best fits the context. Write it in the blank.

1. Figurative language creates _____ pictures in

your mind. It helps you see things in new and unusual ways.

2. Sometimes the _____, or picture, may surprise you. For example,

thinking of a cat as a comma on a rug makes you see the cat in an unexpected way.

3. You can identify a(n) _____ because it always contains the word

like or *as*. When you say, "He is as clever as a fox," you are using this figure of speech.

4. A _____ is more direct. When you say

"He is a fox," you are using a metaphor.

5. "The car hummed happily as we drove along a country road." This is an example of

_____, or making a thing act like a person.

6. _____ language is the opposite of figurative language.

When you use this type of language, you mean exactly what you say.

⭐ **Make a Comparison** Pick two poems that you like. Make a list of the ways they are similar. Do they both use similes, metaphors, and personification? Do they both have rhyme and rhythm? Next, make a list of the ways they are different. Then write a comparison between the two, telling how they are alike and different.

21 **Words About Figurative Language**

Check Your Mastery

Directions Read each item below. Write the vocabulary word that best fits in each sentence.

1. "Her eyes are like stars" is a _____. It makes a comparison using *like* or *as*.
   A. personification   **B.** metaphor   **C.** simile

2. "Her eyes are stars" is a _____. It says that one thing is another.
   A. personification   **B.** metaphor   **C.** simile

3. If you were writing a recipe telling how to make pizza, you would use _____ language instead of figurative language.
   A. literal   **B.** simile   **C.** figure of speech

4. "A flower opened her petals and smiled at me" is an example of _____.
   A. personification   **B.** metaphor   **C.** simile

5. A _____ can be a simile or a metaphor.
   A. literal   **B.** personification   **C.** figure of speech

6. "I'm hungry" is a _____ statement.
   A. figure of speech   **B.** personification   **C.** literal

7. "I'm as hungry as a bear" is a _____.
   A. metaphor   **B.** simile   **C.** personification

8. "Kindness whispered in her ear and told her to help needy people."
This sentence is a figure of speech called a _____.
   A. simile   **B.** metaphor   **C.** personification

9. "She is wearing her heart on her sleeve" is a _____.
   A. figure of speech   **B.** personification   **C.** literal statement

10. "You are my shining star" is a _____.
   A. simile   **B.** metaphor   **C.** personification

Learn Words About a New Subject

Directions Read each test item so that you will recognize how each word might be used in a test. Look at the information after the test item to find out more about the word.

> Read the **passage** below. Then tell the main idea of the **passage**.
>
> *Jimmy's parents bought him a trumpet on his eleventh birthday. As soon as he got the trumpet, he started to practice every day for at least two hours. All the neighbors could hear him playing the same song over and over again. It didn't really bother anyone. In fact, everyone thought it was fantastic that he practiced so hard. And besides, they didn't even have to look at their clocks to know when it was time for dinner. Every night at six o'clock sharp, Jimmy stopped practicing. That meant his mom had called him to come downstairs for dinner!*

A **passage** is a short piece of literature that you read on a test. Some **passages** are fiction. Other **passages** are nonfiction and give interesting facts and information. When you see a **passage** on a test, it means that you will have to tell about the **passage** or answer questions about it.

> **PROMPT:** Choose two folktales from different cultures that explain why people should share. Compare and contrast these two folktales.
>
> In your response, be sure to:
>
> · tell from which two cultures the folktales come
>
> · describe what the folktales mean to you about sharing
>
> · give specific details and examples

A **prompt** on a test tells you how to respond. It describes the writing task and outlines everything you are expected to do to write a good **response**. The **prompt** may give you a topic about which to write, or it may have you choose something to write about. The **prompt** may also ask several questions for you to answer in writing.

(continued on next page)

Vocabulary Words

identify   prompt

insert   response

passage

Word Learning Tip!

When you read about a new subject, you may see words you have not seen before in your everyday reading. These words are often the longest and most difficult in the text. They tell you something specific about the subject. To learn these new words, think about the big idea or subject about which you are reading. In this lesson, all of the words tell about test taking.

Vocabulary Building Strategy

To learn the meaning of content words that tell about a new subject, make connections between the unknown word and the big idea or subject. The new word will tell something specific about that big idea or subject. Tie together the big idea and the meanings of other content words that you know in the text. This will help you determine the exact meaning of the unknown content words.

Learn Words About a New Subject

| identify | insert | passage | prompt | response |

RESPONSE: Both "Anita and the Crows" and "The Secret of Ling" tell about how two families learned to share. They come from Brazil and China. They taught me that it is important to share what I have with people who might have less. You never know when you might be the person who doesn't have enough to eat. In the folktale from Brazil, "Anita and the Crows," at first Anita is very selfish. Then she loses everything she has. Her only friends are the crows, who share food with her. In the Chinese folktale, "The Secret of Ling," Ling's family loses everything in a bad storm. The only family in the village who has anything left is the Lee family. They are the poorest family in the village, but they offer to share what little food they have with Ling's family.

Your **response** is what you write to address the response. The response may consist of your thoughts, opinions, or feelings. It includes information to back up your ideas.

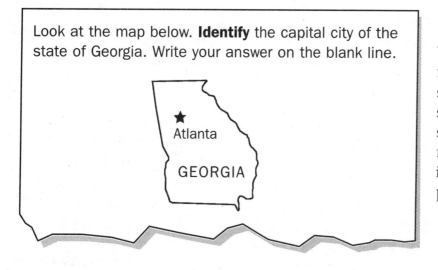

Look at the map below. **Identify** the capital city of the state of Georgia. Write your answer on the blank line.

★
Atlanta

GEORGIA

To **identify** means to recognize or tell what something is, where something is, or who someone is. You might be asked to **identify** a place or a person on a test.

Insert a comma in the correct place in this sentence:

After Bessie Coleman learned to fly she dazzled audiences with her loop-the-loops and figure eights.

Some questions test your knowledge of grammar, usage, and mechanics. To **insert** means to put, or add, something in the correct place. You might be asked to **insert** a punctuation mark or to **insert** words to make a sentence grammatically correct.

Connect Words and Meanings

identify   insert   passage   prompt   response

Directions Read each definition. Circle the letter of the vocabulary word that best fits. You may use a dictionary or the glossary to help you.

1. to tell what something is or who someone is
   A. insert   **B.** response   **C.** identify

2. a writing task outlining what has to be included in a composition
   A. prompt   **B.** passage   **C.** identify

3. what you write as the result of a prompt on a writing test
   A. insert   **B.** identify   **C.** response

4. to add something in the correct place
   A. respond   **B.** insert   **C.** prompt

5. a fictional or informational selection on a test
   A. prompt   **B.** passage   **C.** response

Directions Read the paragraph. Write the vocabulary word that fits best in each blank.

Carmelita looked at the test carefully. On the first page she read a short, nonfiction

(**6**) _____ about Betsy Ross, who made the first American

flag. There were eight multiple-choice questions to answer. One question asked students to

(**7**) _____ the state in which Betsy Ross sewed the first American flag.

On the next page, there was a writing (**8**) _____, or task.

Students were asked to write a composition about what the American flag means to them.

Carmelita really liked the (**9**) _____ she wrote to this task. When

she read it over, she noticed that she had left out a word in one sentence. Carmelita had to

(**10**) _____ the word to correct a grammar error. Then,

her test was complete.

 Write Some Test-Taking Tips Work with a partner. Spend a few minutes brainstorming some useful tips for taking a test. Then write at least five test-taking tips in your personal word journal. Try to include at least three vocabulary words and other test-taking words that you know.

Use Content Words

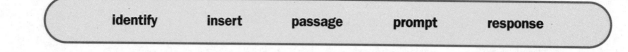

| identify | insert | passage | prompt | response |

Directions Read the following items. Then write the vocabulary word that answers each question. You will use each vocabulary word two times in the activity. Write each word in the blank.

1. A punctuation mark is missing from this sentence. Add it in the correct place. What word describes what you are asked to do?

_____

2. You have just read an article about Lewis and Clark, who were early American explorers. Tell whether you would have liked to be part of their expedition. Why or why not? What form will your answer take? _____

3. Read the following selection:

Every summer, I go to New Hampshire in August so that I can see the shooting stars. August is really the best month to see them. It's a lot of fun to row the boat out to the middle of Lake Winnepesaukee and watch the stars streak across the night sky.

What is another word that means the same as *selection*? _____

4. Choose two songs that make you feel happy. Write about them, using an opening paragraph, a body, and a conclusion. In your response, tell:

- what the songs are
- who the singers are
- why the songs make you happy

What is the above writing task called?

_____

5. Combine these two sentences:

- Put a comma before the word *and*.
- Which vocabulary word describes what you do when you put a comma before the word *and*?

_____

6. Look at the map of the United States. Write the names of the states that border Ohio. What vocabulary word tells what you must do here? _____

⭐ **Write a Prompt** Work with a partner. Select a book you both have read. On a separate piece of paper, write a prompt about this book for a test. Remember to list what you want included in the response.

Put Words Into Action

> identify   insert   passage   prompt   response

Directions Here are some comments that a teacher might write in response to a test you took. Write the vocabulary word that best fits in the blank.

1. This writing task, or _____, asked you to tell where the story took place. You included that information in what you wrote. Good work!

2. Please _____ the capital of Massachusetts. Tell where the capital is located.

3. You've shown that you understood the _____ you read about the Hopi Indians. The information you included in your answer is very interesting.

4. You left out a few words in your _____. Read your answer again to make sure that the grammar and punctuation are correct.

5. You forgot to _____ a comma in this sentence. Otherwise, everything is perfect.

6. This is a very good essay about Benjamin Banneker. You were careful to _____ where he was born and what he did.

7. I really liked your answer, but I want you to rewrite your _____ to also include your opinion about the story. This will make it even better.

8. Reread your test answers to make sure that you didn't leave out any other words. If you did, make sure that you _____ them in the correct place.

9. Reread this informational _____ about San Francisco. Then choose a different answer.

10. You did a very nice job of answering each part of the _____, or task, but you didn't proofread what you wrote. Please take a few minutes to reread this and make any necessary changes.

⭐ **Write a Test With a Partner** Work with a partner. Brainstorm some questions you might include on a test. Write the questions in your personal word journal. Use all vocabulary words and two other test-taking words that you know. Your questions should be about a subject you've studied this week at school.

Review and Extend

| identify | insert | passage | prompt | response |

BONUS WORDS Here are two new test-taking words. Remember that these words all deal with the same big idea as your vocabulary words. That means that even if you have never seen these words before, you know that they have to do with taking tests. You can use what you already know about taking tests to understand the meaning of these words.

connect to link two or more things

express to show what you feel or think by saying, doing, or writing something

Directions Read each item below. Choose the vocabulary word or bonus word that best fits. Write it in the blank.

1. This test item asks you to _____ your thoughts about friendship by stating in writing what you think and feel.

2. Another test item asks you to _____ two sentences using the word *because*.

3. Be careful to _____ a comma between two complete thoughts in a sentence.

4. Can you _____ the names of the countries that border Switzerland?

5. After you look at the writing task described in the _____, write your composition on the lines below it.

6. This direction line asks you to read the _____ and then answer questions about it.

7. After you read the prompt on the test, think about the points that you must address in your _____.

8. Read this informational _____ about hurricanes and then write a short paragraph that tells what you learned.

⭐ **Write Test Questions** In your personal word journal, write a short paragraph about a topic you know something about. It can be about a favorite book, an animal, a sport, or any other topic you like. Write three test questions for the passage.

Check Your Mastery

Directions Read each item below. Circle the letter of the vocabulary word that best fits in each sentence.

1. The first _____ in the test is a short story. Read it and then answer the multiple-choice questions.
   A. prompt   **B.** passage   **C.** insert

2. Another question asks you to _____ the two countries that border the United States.
   A. identify   **B.** insert   **C.** response

3. One of the test items has missing punctuation marks. Your job is to _____ them around the author's exact words.
   A. identify   **B.** response   **C.** insert

4. The last test item is a writing _____. It asks you to write a composition about two sea creatures that you find scary.
   A. prompt   **B.** passage   **C.** response

5. For test item 4, your _____ must include your opinion about space travel.
   A. prompt   **B.** response   **C.** insert

6. When you read an informational _____, think about how the facts fit together.
   A. prompt   **B.** passage   **C.** response

7. You may be asked to _____ the main idea. The facts must fit this main idea.
   A. prompt   **B.** insert   **C.** identify

8. On some tests, you may have to read a poem and discuss what the poem means in your _____.
   A. response   **B.** identify   **C.** insert

9. The grammar section of a test might ask you to _____ words to make a sentence complete.
   A. response   **B.** passage   **C.** insert

10. This _____ asks you to compare and contrast two characters from your favorite book.
   A. prompt   **B.** response   **C.** identify

CHAPTER **4**

Words and Their Histories

23 Words From Other Languages

Read Words in Context

READ!

Vocabulary Words

avocado	kebab
banana	macaroni
bologna	pasta
coffee	pickle
cole slaw	spaghetti
curry	strudel
frankfurter	tofu
hamburger	

Word Learning Tip!

Some words in our language look or sound different because they were first used in another language or country. We "borrowed" these words and use them in the English language. Knowing a word's history can help you understand its meaning. The words in this lesson all name foods that came from other countries and languages.

Vocabulary Building Strategy

Use Word History The words in this lesson name foods that come from Spanish, Italian, German, Japanese, and even the ancient Aztec Indians' language. Picture each food in your mind. Think about where it came from and link the picture and place with the name of the food. This can help you understand the word's meaning.

A World of Food Treats

Which do you like better—a **frankfurter** or a **hamburger**? You may think these are all-American meats. But they are not. Frankfurters and hamburgers came from Germany. Frankfurters are named after the city of Frankfurt, Germany. Hamburgers come from the German city of Hamburg. Do you eat **bologna** sandwiches? This meat product comes from Italy. It was named after the Italian city of Bologna.

Another favorite American food is **spaghetti**. It also comes from Italy. It is a form of **pasta**, a food made from flour and water. Pasta comes in many shapes and sizes. **Macaroni** is pasta cut into small, fat tubes.

From the late 1500s on, European explorers sailed to lands that were new to them. They brought back from Africa the yellow fruit that hangs from trees and kept its African name—**banana**. They brought **curry** from India and kept its Indian name. This spice mixture was used to make meat and vegetable dishes. **Coffee**, a hot or cold strong-tasting drink, and **kebabs**, meat or vegetables cooked on a stick, came from Turkey. Spanish explorers returned from Mexico with **avocados,** a green fruit that we eat very much like a vegetable. **Tofu**—a soft food made from soybeans—is from China and Japan. We kept its name, although we changed its spelling and pronunciation a bit.

Some foods came to the United States with early settlers who used the words from their native lands. The Dutch put vegetables in vinegar or salt and water so they would not spoil. A cucumber that has been preserved in vinegar or salt is called a **pickle** after the Dutch word *pekel*. **Cole slaw** is a salad of shredded cabbage and mayonnaise. It comes from the Dutch word *koolsla*. **Strudel** is a German word that names a tasty German pastry with a fruit or cheese filling. The original German word meant "whirlpool." When you taste strudel, do you feel a whirlpool of tasty delights on your tongue?

Connect Words and Meanings

avocado	coffee	frankfurter	macaroni	spaghetti
banana	cole slaw	hamburger	pasta	strudel
bologna	curry	kebab	pickle	tofu

Directions Read the definition of each word and its history. Then choose the vocabulary word that fits in the blank. You may use the dictionary or the glossary to help you.

1. **Definition:** a green, pear-shaped fruit with a large pit
   History: The word comes from the Aztecs of Mexico by way of the Spanish. Nilda made a salad with lettuce, tomato, and _____.

2. **Definition:** a noodle made of flour and water
   History: The name of this food comes from the Italian language. It adds the meaning "little" to the word *spago*, which means "small cord."
   _____ comes in long, thin sticks that you boil.

3. **Definition:** a mixture of hot spices in a dish of meat and vegetables
   History: This word comes from India. The original word was *kari*.
   The _____ at the Indian restaurant had a spicy yellow sauce.

4. **Definition:** a pastry made of dough and a sweet filling of fruit or cheese
   History: The word for this dessert comes to us from the German language and means "whirlpool." It is related to the German word *stredan*, meaning "to bubble."
   The warm apple _____ made a wonderful dessert.

5. **Definition:** a meat patty
   History: This food gets its name from a city in Germany called Hamburg.
   Do you want your _____ with or without fries?

6. **Definition:** a bland, cheeselike food made from soybeans that is rich in protein
   History: This word comes from the Chinese and Japanese languages. It is made up of two smaller words, *dou*, which means "bean," and *fu*, which means "rot."
   The hot-and-sour soup contained _____ as well as vegetables.

7. **Definition:** a dark-brown drink made by brewing roasted, beanlike seeds in water
   History: This word comes from the Turkish language. It is based on the name of the area in Ethiopia, *Kaff*, where the plant grows.
   Dad always puts milk in his
   _____.

8. **Definition:** a long, curved, yellow tropical fruit
   History: This word comes from West Africa, where the word looks very much the same. The Spanish and Portuguese brought it into the English language.
   Keisha sliced a _____ and placed it on top of her ice cream.

(continued on next page)

Connect More Words and Meanings

avocado	coffee	frankfurter	macaroni	spaghetti
banana	cole slaw	hamburger	pasta	strudel
bologna	curry	kebab	pickle	tofu

Directions Match each food in the left-hand column with its definition in the right-hand column. Write the letter of the correct definition on the blank by the word. You may use a dictionary or the glossary to help you.

9. _____ cole slaw   **A.** a hot dog named after the town of Frankfurt, in Germany

10. _____ frankfurter   **B.** a smoked sausage named after an Italian city

11. _____ macaroni   **C.** a hot drink with a Turkish name; its name may have come from Kaff, Ethiopia

12. _____ kebab   **D.** a side dish made with shredded cabbage; from the Dutch word *koolsla*

13. _____ spaghetti   **E.** a meat patty named after a German city

14. _____ coffee   **F.** short, hollow tubes of pasta; from the Italian word *maccaroni*

15. _____ tofu   **G.** a cucumber soaked in salty water; from the Dutch word *pekel*, meaning a mix of salt and water

16. _____ bologna   **H.** long, thin sticks of pasta; from the Italian word *spago* plus the ending for "little"

17. _____ banana   **I.** meat or vegetables cooked on a stick; a Turkish treat from the word *kabāb*

18. _____ pickle   **J.** a Chinese/Japanese word for bean curd, made up of the words *dou* and *fu*

19. _____ hamburger   **K.** a green, pear-shaped fruit that came from Mexico; some people call it "alligator pear"

20. _____ avocado   **L.** a yellow fruit with an African name

⭐ **Find Other Foreign Words** Each week, new words are added to the English language. Read a newspaper, magazine, or textbook for 20 minutes. Find three words that look or sound as if they came from another language. Write the sentence in which you found them and what you think they mean. Check a dictionary to see if you are correct.

Use Words in Context

avocado	coffee	frankfurter	macaroni	spaghetti
banana	cole slaw	hamburger	pasta	strudel
bologna	curry	kebab	pickle	tofu

Directions Read each sentence below. Write the vocabulary word(s) that best fits in the sentence.

1. Our school had a Foods of the World Fair. One family made a food that had meat and vegetables on a metal stick. They put these _____(s) on a grill and cooked them.

2. Mr. and Mrs. Bergen made a pastry that had two fruits in it. Everyone wanted a piece of this tasty dessert called _____.

3. At a booth called "Little Italy," you could eat macaroni, spaghetti, and other _____ dishes.

4. Mr. and Mrs. Tanaka showed our class how to prepare a spicy bean-curd recipe with _____.

5. Some summertime picnic favorites were served, too. Although these dishes seem "all American," they are named after two cities in Germany. They were _____.

Directions Answer each of the questions with a complete sentence containing a vocabulary word. Do not use a vocabulary word more than once. Write your answers on the blank line.

6. Which one of these foods would you like to eat at a picnic? _____
_____

7. Which one of these foods would you like to eat for lunch at home? _____
_____

8. Which one of these foods would grown-ups like more than kids? _____
_____

⭐ **Find Names of Cars** Several cars have names that originally came from other countries. Write the names of two cars that you think may be a word from another language. Tell how the Word Learning Tip and Vocabulary Building Strategy can help you learn the meaning of words that name new cars, inventions, and products.

23 Words From Other Languages

Put Words Into Action

avocado	coffee	frankfurter	macaroni	spaghetti
banana	cole slaw	hamburger	pasta	strudel
bologna	curry	kebab	pickle	tofu

Directions Below are menus from different restaurants. Think about the origin of each vocabulary word. Then write the word on the correct menu.

Italy

1. _____
2. _____
3. _____
4. _____

Germany

5. _____
6. _____
7. _____

Holland (Dutch)

8. _____
9. _____

Turkey

10. _____
11. _____

Africa

12. _____

India

13. _____

China and Japan

14. _____

Mexico

15. _____

 Learn a Word History Choose one of the following names of a food—guacamole, tamales, sushi, ketchup, papaya, tomatoes—or select a different food. Find out about its history. You may use the dictionary, a reference book from the library, or the Internet to help you. Tell the history of your word in a paragraph, in a comic strip, or in pictures.

Review and Extend

avocado	coffee	frankfurter	macaroni	spaghetti
banana	cole slaw	hamburger	pasta	strudel
bologna	curry	kebab	pickle	tofu

BONUS WORDS Here are some Spanish food words and their histories.

Barbecue meat cooked with a spicy sauce on an outdoor grill. **Barbecue** comes from the Spanish name for the grill that the meat is cooked on. The word originally came from the Taino Indians of the Caribbean, who were conquered by the Spaniards.

Salsa a spicy tomato sauce flavored with onions and peppers. **Salsa** is a Spanish word. It comes from the Latin word for salt. Latin was the language of the ancient Romans. Salt was used by the Romans to flavor food and keep it from spoiling.

Directions Replace the underlined words in each sentence with the correct vocabulary or bonus word. Write the word in the blank.

1. We went to a restaurant that served <u>meat with a spicy sauce cooked over a fire</u>. This food has a Spanish name. _____

2. <u>A spicy tomato sauce</u> from Mexico went well with our burritos. _____

3. <u>The special mixture of spices from India</u> gave the dish a delicious flavor. _____

4. Consuela ate <u>meat and vegetables on a stick</u>. This is a favorite food in Turkey, Israel, Egypt, and other countries in the Middle East. _____

5. Doreen asked for a <u>cucumber soaked in vinegar</u>. She liked having this along with with her cheese sandwich. _____

6. Evan likes <u>noodles made from flour and water</u>. "I'll take any kind," he said, "spaghetti, macaroni, rigatoni, ravioli, or whatever other kind you have." _____

7. The name for <u>shredded cabbage salad</u> comes from the Dutch word *koolsla*. "It goes well with potato salad and sandwiches," said Kevin. _____

8. "I'll have some with my <u>smoked sausage</u> and cheese sandwich," Carla remarked.

    _____

9. In Italian it's called *caffe*. In French, it's called *cafe*. Most of the time, adults in this country order it by its American name. _____

10. Lance made a <u>dessert with a cheese filling</u>. "Save room for it," he said. _____

⭐ **Search for New Words From Other Languages** Work with a partner to make a list of words for foods from other languages. Think of some words from the Spanish language for Mexican foods and from Italian, Chinese, and Japanese languages for foods from these countries. Also think of names of foods American Indians gave us.

Check Your Mastery

Directions Read the following sentences. Circle the letter of the word that best answers the question or completes the statement.

1. If you ate a Japanese soup with bean curd, it would contain:

   A. coffee   **B.** tofu   **C.** avocado

2. If you like baked apples in a fluffy pastry crust, this is just the dessert for you.

   A. strudel   **B.** banana   **C.** pickle

3. Which food is NOT a kind of pasta?

   A. macaroni   **B.** spaghetti   **C.** cole slaw

4. People drink this beverage in the morning, although in some parts of the world they prefer tea.

   A. coffee   **B.** bologna   **C.** tofu

5. If you are hungry for a type of sausage on a roll with mustard, you would order this.

   A. hamburger   **B.** frankfurter   **C.** strudel

6. You have finished your sandwich and you don't want dessert. What might you pick up from the side of your dish to eat?

   A. pickle   **B.** strudel   **C.** bologna

7. When some people eat this, they take the meat and vegetables from the stick.

   A. cole slaw   **B.** kebab   **C.** curry

8. This yellow fruit has a peel that you must take off in order to eat.

   A. avocado   **B.** banana   **C.** hamburger

9. If you go to an Indian restaurant, you might order this.

   A. banana   **B.** hamburger   **C.** curry

10. This green fruit has a delicious taste and it's also used in creams and lotions.

    A. avocado   **B.** macaroni   **C.** pickle

Read Words in Context

READ!

Buster's Rescue

"Did you know that a **horse** can talk?" asked Jared. "Watch Starbuck eat from that **bale** of hay. See how he **chews**. Now he draws back his lips and says, 'Neigh.'"

"But that means no more than a bird saying, '**Cheep, cheep,**'" I reply.

"Moon Shadow's nudging Starbuck to get at the food. Listen to Starbuck squeal at the other horse. That squeal is a warning signal that says, 'Stay away' or 'Watch out.'" explained Jared.

"Let's walk down the **aisle** between the stalls. **Choose** a seat. Pull up one of those old chairs. I want to tell you a story." said Jared.

"Every horse has its own special whinny or neigh. When I hear you speak, I can recognize you by your voice. I can even tell it's you when your voice is a little **hoarse** from a cold. Horses can recognize one another by the sound of their whinnies and neighs. They can hear this sound from half a mile away.

"Last year I brought Moon Shadow and her foal, Buster, to a horse show on Greenwood Island. Of course, you know that a foal is a baby horse. The first night there, I rowed out to watch the sunset. The sunset was beautiful, but I had some trouble with the boat. It was a pretty **cheap** rowboat, though, not at all an expensive one. I had to **bail** water for most of the night because the boat leaked so badly.

"The next day, Buster got lost. Moon Shadow whinnied, calling for her child. Her ears pricked up when she heard an answering neigh. Off she ran, with us following, until she brought us right to where Buster was trapped by a fallen tree."

"After we freed the foal, Moon Shadow and Buster nickered gently. Horses make this soft sound to greet one another. A mare uses it to tell its foal to stay close."

I laughed, "**I'll** bet Moon Shadow nickered the rest of the time you spent on the **isle**."

Vocabulary Words

aisle/I'll/isle
bail/bale
cheap/cheep
chews/choose
hoarse/horse

Word Learning Tip!

English words come from many other languages. Some English words are pronounced the same but are spelled differently and have different meanings. Although they sound the same, they are really two different words.

Vocabulary Building Strategy

When words sound alike but are spelled differently and have different meanings, they are easy to confuse. Think about the context of the sentence to determine the correct homophone. You can also look at how the word is spelled. Both of these strategies can help you to determine the meaning of the word and how it is used in the sentence.

Connect Words and Meanings

| aisle/I'll/isle | bail/bale | cheap/cheep | chews/choose | hoarse/horse |

Directions Circle the letter in front of the word in each pair of homophones that fits the definition. You may use a dictionary or your glossary to help you.

1. to make a sound like a baby bird; from a Scottish word that imitates the sound of a bird
   A. cheap   **B.** cheep

2. to scoop water out of a boat; from an Old French word for bucket; the word also means a sum of money paid to get someone out of jail
   A. bale   **B.** bail

3. a rough, husky voice; from the Middle English word *hors*
   A. horse   **B.** hoarse

4. an island; from the French word *ile,* for island
   A. aisle   **B.** isle

5. to pick out something or someone from among several; from a Middle English word that meant "to split"
   A. choose   **B.** chews

6. not costing very much; from the Old English word meaning "not expensive, a bargain"
   A. cheep   **B.** cheap

7. a bundle of something tied up tightly, such as hay or straw; from an Old French word meaning "ball"
   A. bale   **B.** bail

8. grinds food with its teeth; from an Old English word meaning "to bite"
   A. choose   **B.** chews

9. a pathway between seats in a theater or train; from the French word *ele,* meaning "a wing of a building"
   A. aisle   **B.** isle

10. a large animal with hooves that people ride; from the Middle English word *hors,* which split into two different words forming two homophones
    A. horse   **B.** hoarse

 Play a Word Game Your teacher will hand out flashcards with a word on one side and a definition on the other. Take turns. Shuffle the cards, and then put the cards face down. Each player takes a card from the pile and makes up a sentence for that word. If the player uses the word incorrectly, he or she gives the card to the other player. Keep playing until you have made up a sentence for each card.

Use Words in Context

aisle/I'll/isle   bail/bale   cheap/cheep   chews/choose   hoarse/horse

Directions Read each pair of sentences. Write the correct vocabulary word in each blank.

1. Mandy said to Gina, "Let's walk down the _____ (*aisle, I'll, isle*)

and find seats for the movie."

2. We want to have good seats to see *The* _____ (*Aisle, I'll, Isle*)

of Pink Shells and Coconuts.

3. Stella _____ (*chews, choose*) her nails when she is nervous.

4. She gets nervous when she has to _____ (*chews, choose*)

an answer on a test.

5. Cody spent a lot of time in the barn treating his _____

(*hoarse, horse*) for a bruised leg.

6. Yesterday he caught a cold and now his voice is _____

(*hoarse, horse*).

7. Terrell put a _____ (*bail, bale*) of hay out for the horse to eat.

8. The man paid _____ (*bail, bale*) to get his friend out of jail.

9. A _____ (*cheap, cheep*) way to get fresh eggs is to raise chickens.

10. You can listen to the baby chicks _____ (*cheap, cheep*)

as they run around the barnyard.

· ·

⭐ **Combine Two Homophones** Work with a partner. Think of a way to combine a set of two homophones in one or two sentences. For example, you might write: "Lisa got *hoarse* calling out to the *horse* to come back to her." Use your imagination and make up sentences of your own using all the homophones from the vocabulary list.

Put Words Into Action

> aisle/I'll/isle   bail/bale   cheap/cheep   chews/choose   hoarse/horse

Directions Read each question. Write an answer for each question that uses the boldface word. Write the answer on the line.

1. How can you avoid getting **hoarse**? _____

2. What are two items that you might be able to buy at a **cheap** price? _____

_____

3. Why do you think that hay is packed in a **bale**? _____

4 What can you use to **bail** out a boat? _____

5. What animals **cheep**? _____

6. What are some things that a boy **chews**? _____

7. If you could own a **horse**, where would you ride it? _____

8. If you could pick a place to visit, what place would you **choose**? _____

_____

9. Where would you most likely find an **aisle**? _____

_____

10. When you say, "**I'll** do it!" do you mean that you already did something or that you will

do something? _____

⭐ **Make a Homophone Chart** Work with a partner to make a list of the homophones you know on a separate piece of paper. Remember that the words must sound alike but have different meanings and spellings. Make two columns for your chart. At the top of one column write Words and at the top of the other write Meanings. Put your words and their definitions on your chart.

Review and Extend

aisle/I'll/isle   bail/bale   cheap/cheep   chews/choose   hoarse/horse

BONUS WORDS Here are some other homophones that sound alike but are spelled differently and have different meanings. They also have different word histories.

mail/male *Mail* means "letters and packages" and comes from a French word for the bag that was used to carry mail. *Male* is used to describe masculine people and animals. The word came into English from French.

root/route A *root* is the underground part of a plant. It comes from an Old English word. A *route* can be a road or the usual path someone or something takes. *Route* comes from a French word for road. An example is the route the school bus takes to school. *Route* is a homophone for *root* when it is pronounced /root/, but some people pronounce it /rout/.

Directions Read each sentence. Look at the word(s) in boldface. In the blank, write the correct vocabulary or bonus word that could replace the word(s) in boldface.

1. Dad drives to work along the same **road** every day. _____

2. The computer was on sale for a **very low** price. _____

3. Only one kitten in the litter was a **boy**. The others were all females. _____

4. The gardener pulled the **bottom part** of the plant out of the ground. _____

5. One **package** of straw sat alone in the back of the truck. _____

6. **I will** bring a present to Mike's birthday party. _____

7. How am I going to **pick** just one of these great T-shirts to buy? _____

8. After giving a long speech, the candidate's voice sounded **rough and sore**. _____

9. The office is waiting for important **letters and packages**. _____

10. When waves splashed into the boat, we had **to scoop out** the water. _____

⭐ **Write Movie Titles** With a partner, brainstorm some ideas for four movie titles and directors' names. Choose four vocabulary words—one for each title. Then make up a director's name for each title that has good context clues for each vocabulary word you chose. For example, "The *Route* to Apache Junction!" By Robbie Road. Write the movie titles in your personal word journal.

Check Your Mastery

Directions Read the questions. Circle the letter of the best answer to each question.

1. Which of the following might make someone **hoarse**?

   A. shouting   **B.** riding   **C.** playing baseball

2. Which of the following would say "**cheep**"?

   A. a puppy   **B.** a baby bird   **C.** a store owner

3. Which of the following might be in **bales** stacked in a barn?

   A. water   **B.** honey   **C.** hay

4. Which of the following has the same meaning as "**I will** pick"?

   A. Isle choose   **B.** I'll chews   **C.** I'll choose

5. Which of the following might you have to **bail** out?

   A. a boat   **B.** a bicycle   **C.** a skateboard

6. Which of these has the same meaning as *island*?

   A. aisle   **B.** I'll   **C.** isle

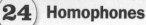

7. Which of the following is LEAST likely to be **cheap**?

   A. shoes   **B.** a computer   **C.** a book

8. Which of the following is something a horse **chews**?

   A. carrots   **B.** pebbles   **C.** water

9. Which of the following would be found on a train?

   A. aisle   **B.** isle   **C.** I'll

10. Which of the following phrases is correct?

   A. a bail of string   **B.** a cheep car   **C.** a bale of hay

Read Words in Context

Griots: Keepers of History

Some stories have been passed along orally from one generation to another. They have not been written down. In Africa, special people have been given the honor of retelling the stories of their ancestors. They are called griots (GREE-oz).

Long ago, griots were advisors to the kings of the great empire of Mali. Today, they still perform important tasks by giving **advice** to people in their community. Their most important job, though, is to retell the ancient stories of their ancestors.

Griots tell different kinds of stories to help them inform and entertain people. Sometimes they tell trickster tales to **advise** people about what is right or wrong. They also share myths to explain **customs** that are part of their community. Griots might even dress in a **costume** to portray a certain character. Good stories can **affect**, or influence, how people live.

The griots' stories and songs have a strong **effect** on people. Sometimes, the listeners **suspect** that parts of the stories are not exactly true. Even so, they don't want to **lose** the stories of their past, so it's not important to them that every detail is accurate.

For entertainment, the audience **expects** griots to "raise a song" so the community can respond. This is called "call and response." When griots sing a song-tale, they play stringed instruments that they pluck, and they wear long, **loose** robes. Griots have been retelling stories for hundreds of years now. The art of storytelling remains a beautiful living tradition in Africa and other places.

Vocabulary Words

advice/advise
affect/effect
costume/custom
expect/suspect
loose/lose

Word Learning Tip!

Sometimes words are easy to confuse because they sound almost alike. However, they have very different meanings. The two easily confused words may have come from different languages. Or, they may have come from the same word, but as their pronunciations started to change, so did their meanings.

Vocabulary Building Strategy

It is sometimes easy to confuse words because they sound similar, but remember their meanings are always different. One way to tell the difference between words that are easily confused is to look at the context in which a word is used. Then create a clue tied to the spelling of the word to help you remember that word's meaning.

Connect Words and Meanings

advice/advise   affect/effect   costume/custom   expect/suspect   loose/lose

Directions Choose the correct vocabulary word for each definition. Write it in the blank.

1. **Definition:** to influence people, or to change someone or something (borrowed from the Latin word *affectare*, meaning "to exert influence") _____ (effect, affect)

2. **Definition:** to think that something ought to happen (borrowed from the Latin word *expectare*, meaning "to hope or to look for") _____ (suspect, expect)

3. **Definition:** not fastened or attached firmly (borrowed from the old Norse word *lauss*) _____ (lose, loose)

4. **Definition:** clothes worn for some purpose or occasion (borrowed from the Old French and Italian word *costume*, meaning "fashion or habit") _____ (costume, custom)

5. **Definition:** to give someone a suggestion about what to do (borrowed from the Old French *avis*, meaning "opinion") _____ (advise, advice)

6. **Definition:** to think something might be true (borrowed from the Latin word *suspicere*, meaning to "to look under") _____ (suspect, expect)

7. **Definition:** a tradition in a culture or society (borrowed from the Latin word *cōnsuētūdō*, meaning "habit") _____ (costume, custom)

8. **Definition:** a suggestion about what someone should do (borrowed from the Old French phrase *a vis*, meaning "opinion") _____ (advice, advise)

9. **Definition:** the result or consequence of something (borrowed from the Latin word *effectus*, meaning "result or completion") _____ (affect, effect)

10. **Definition:** to not have something anymore (developed from the Old English word *losian*, meaning "to lose") _____ (lose, loose)

. . . .

⭐ **Write a Trickster Tale** Work with a partner. Brainstorm a clever animal character for your story. For example, you might want to use a tortoise, an owl, or a mosquito! Then discuss how the animal character *advises* people about something that is right or wrong. Write the story in your personal word journal. Use at least six vocabulary words in your tale.

Use Words in Context

advice/advise   affect/effect   costume/custom   expect/suspect   loose/lose

Directions Choose the correct word to complete each sentence. Write the word in the blank.

1. Margot doesn't want to _____ (*loose/lose*) any of the beads on the antique dress.

2. The dress is very old, so many of the beads are _____ (*loose/lose*).

3. Because the new coach _____ (ed) (*affect/effect*) the team in a positive way, it had a winning season.

4. The _____ (*affect/effect*), or result, of the teacher's new grading system was that a student could earn bonus points.

5. Abraham Lincoln made Thanksgiving a national holiday on October 3, 1863. Through the years, celebrating Thanksgiving has become a favorite _____ (*costume/custom*) of many people.

6. Carmelo thought it was fun to wear a _____ (*costume/custom*) to the party.

7. Leah didn't _____ (*expect/suspect*) that so many people would come to her concert.

8. She didn't _____ (*expect/suspect*) that her mother had invited many of the people.

9. "What would you _____ (*advice/advise*) me to do regarding that problem?" asked Jermaine.

10. Can you give me some good _____ (*advice/advise*) about what to tell him?" asked Maya.

⋆ **Write About a Custom in the United States** Work with a partner. Talk about some *customs* that people follow in the United States. Make a list in your personal word journal. Then choose a *custom* where people might wear *costumes*. Write about a *costume* that you might wear to celebrate the *custom*. Use all the vocabulary words in your description.

Put Words Into Action

advice/advise   affect/effect   costume/custom   expect/suspect   loose/lose

Directions Read each sentence. If the boldface vocabulary word is not used correctly in the sentence, write the correct word in the blank. If the word is correct, write correct.

1. Mariko wore a Japanese **custom** to the party. _____

2. A coach should **advice** players on how to be better in a sport. _____

3. How did the book **affect** you? Did it make you feel happy? _____

4. Be careful not to **loose** your sunglasses. _____

5. "I **suspect** you to review all the notes you took," said Mr. Wang. _____

6. Jeremy's favorite **custom** is the West Indian Parade
that happens every September. _____

7. "Be careful! The hinges on the door are **lose**," said DeeDee. _____

8. "What **affect** will the snowstorm have on our trip?"
Deanna asked. "Will we still be able to go to the play?" _____

9. "I **expect** everyone to turn in their assignments on time,"
said Mr. Gee. _____

10. "Please **advice** us of your plans when you know them,"
Mrs. Knight said. _____

⭐ **Write Mixed-Up Sentences** Write six sentences on a separate piece of paper. In some sentences, use the correct vocabulary word. In other sentences, use the word with which it is easily confused. Exchange your sentences with another student, and challenge him or her to find the mixed-up word, cross it out, and write the correct word. For example, "The *advise* that Brittany gave her brother was very helpful." *Advise* should be *advice*.

Review and Extend

> advice/advise   affect/effect   costume/custom   expect/suspect   loose/lose

BONUS WORDS Here are some other words that are easily confused. Even though they sound very similar, they are spelled differently and have different meanings.

Word	Meaning	Sentence
lay	to put or to place	Lay the coats on the bench.
lie	to get into or be in a flat position	Lie down on the blanket.

Directions Read each sentence. Choose the vocabulary word or bonus word that best fits and write it in the blank.

1. Rosalinda took off her wet raincoat. "Don't _____ (lie, lay) it on the chair," said her mother.

2. Matt was feeling sick. "I think I'd better _____ (lie, lay) down," he told his brother.

3. Moving away from the old neighborhood had a big _____ (affect, effect) on Tim. He missed his friends a lot.

4. The job of a school counselor is to _____ (advice, advise) students about how to deal with problems.

5. The bus comes to this bus stop every ten minutes. I _____ (expect, suspect) that a bus will come very soon.

6. If you keep a lot of change in your pockets, you may _____ (loose, lose) some of it.

7. It is a _____ (custom, costume) in the United States to celebrate the Fourth of July.

8. Ming liked the _____ (advice, advise) that Coach Murphy gave her about her gymnastics program.

★ **Create Word-Reminder Tips** Work with a partner. Brainstorm some ideas for two tips that might help you not confuse these vocabulary words. What techniques could you use to memorize the words so you don't confuse them? Write the tips in your personal word journal. For example, here's a tip for *loose* and *lose*: Remember that the word *lose* has lost one of its o's.

25 Easily Confused Words

Check Your Mastery

Directions Read each sentence. Write the correct word in the blank.

1. Rhea took her friend's _____ (*advise, advice*) and studied for the test.

2. The big blizzard last night had a huge _____ (*affect, effect*) on my going to school today.

3. My favorite _____ (*costume, custom*) is watching the fireworks on the Fourth of July.

4. I _____ (*suspect, expect*) that Sally is having a party because I hear a lot of talking and music.

5. My little sister has a _____ (*lose, loose*) tooth that will probably fall out in a day or two.

6. What might you _____ (*suspect, expect*) to happen when those two teams play against each other in the soccer tournament?

7. Darcy plans to wear an elephant _____ (*costume, custom*) to the parade.

8. How do you think your sister's decision will _____ (*affect, effect*) the horse's training?

9. Maury called Nellie to _____ (*advice, advise*) her that the band would rehearse at 3 o'clock on Wednesday.

10. Dwight doesn't want to _____ (*loose, lose*) the stamps, so he puts them in his back pocket.

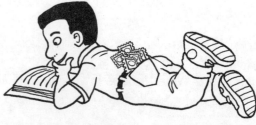

Read Words in Context

READ!

Lights! Camera! Action!

Elvira couldn't believe it! She got the part. For two weeks, the movie director hadn't been able to make up his mind between two people. He had been **sitting on the fence** about picking her. Elvira really wanted the role of the famous comic. It **fit like a glove**. What a perfect match! At the tryout, the director really liked her jokes. He could barely **keep a straight face** when she told the joke about the elephants.

On the first day of rehearsals, Elvira **got off to a flying start**. The director enjoyed her songs. The crew laughed at all her jokes. Elvira was thrilled, but the afternoon rehearsal was a disaster. She forgot the words to her songs. Even worse, she sang off-key, and her tap-dance routine was the biggest disaster of all.

The director was impatient. If she didn't improve, he might regret his choice. Elvira would be **in the doghouse**. She thought that she might get fired, and, if she did, she didn't know how she'd **make ends meet**. She didn't have much money saved. Of course, she did have her part-time job at the theater. "**Half a loaf is better than none,**" her cousin Tasha always said.

She was sure that she was going to have to **face the music** any moment, and she didn't mean facing her songs. She thought the director might replace her. A few minutes later, the director said: "Five-minute break!"

Elvira walked over to Melissa, the makeup artist, to get a retouch. "Listen, Elvira, you made one mistake and then a lot of mistakes followed. Sometimes **when it rains it pours**. It's your first day. It'll work out."

"Thanks!" said Elvira. "Also, I think that I'll just try to remember that **lightning never strikes twice**!"

Guess what? It didn't. After the break, Elvira sang every song well and danced every step perfectly for the rest of the day!

Vocabulary Words

- face the music
- fit like a glove
- get off to a flying start
- half a loaf is better than none
- in the doghouse
- keep a straight face
- lightning never strikes twice
- make ends meet
- sit on the fence
- when it rains, it pours

Word Learning Tip!

An idiom is an expression that means something different from what the individual words normally mean. When the words are put together, they are an imaginative way of expressing an idea. For example, to "sit on the fence" means to "not make up your mind." Remember the meaning of "sit on the fence" by imagining a person sitting on a fence, unable to decide which side of the fence to climb down.

Vocabulary Building Strategy

An idiom is a group of words with a special meaning that may have been created a long time ago. To determine the meaning of an idiom, think about the overall picture that the words could communicate.

Connect Words and Meanings

- face the music
- fit like a glove
- get off to a flying start
- half a loaf is better than none
- in the doghouse

- keep a straight face
- lightning never strikes twice
- make ends meet
- sit on the fence
- when it rains, it pours

Directions Read the definition for each idiom in the column on the right. Write the idiom that best fits the meaning in the blank. Use the glossary to help you.

_____ **1.** better to have something rather than nothing

_____ **2.** when one thing starts to happen, everything starts to happen

_____ **3.** something is a perfect match or suits you

_____ **4.** to not be able to make up your mind

_____ **5.** in trouble or in a bad spot

_____ **6.** to have a good beginning

_____ **7.** something unusual that happened once won't happen again in exactly the same way

_____ **8.** to not show what you're really feeling; stop yourself from laughing

_____ **9.** to confront an unpleasant situation; accept punishment or harsh words

_____ **10.** to live within one's income or means; make and spend the amount of money that you have

Create Idiom Tips Work in small groups. Choose three idioms. Write them on separate paper. Come up with three tips that might help you remember what these idioms mean. For example, picture in your mind what it looks like when rain pours down heavily. Think of a tip you could use to remember *when it rains, it pours.*

Use Words in Context

> - face the music
> - fit like a glove
> - get off to a flying start
> - half a loaf is better than none
> - in the doghouse
>
> - keep a straight face
> - lightning never strikes twice
> - make ends meet
> - sit on the fence
> - when it rains, it pours

Directions Read each question. Think about the imaginative meaning of the idiom. Then write your answer on the blank line. Remember to write complete sentences, and include the idiom in your answer.

1. Do you think it is true that **lightning doesn't strike twice**? Why or why not?

   _____

2. When have you found it hard to **keep a straight face**?

   _____

3. What hobby or sport do you like that **fits you like a glove**?

   _____

4. Why would you not want to be **in the doghouse**?

   _____

5. What is an example of **half a loaf being better than none**?

   _____

6. What does it usually mean when someone has to **face the music**?

   _____

7. Why is it important to **make ends meet**? _____

8. If someone is new at a school, how could he or she get **off to a flying start**?

   _____

9. In what situation might you use the idiom **when it rains, it pours**?

   _____

10. Do you think it is a good idea or a bad idea to **sit on the fence** when you have
    to make a decision? _____

⭐ **Play Idiom Charades** Break into teams. Write the idioms on a piece of paper and put them in a bowl. Ask a volunteer from each team to pick an idiom. Point out that there are many hand gestures and pantomime movements that lend themselves to these particular idioms. Take some time to decide how your group is going to act out the idiom. Then take turns acting out your idioms for the class.

Put Words Into Action

- face the music
- fit like a glove
- get off to a flying start
- half a loaf is better than none
- in the doghouse
- keep a straight face
- lightning never strikes twice
- make ends meet
- sit on the fence
- when it rains, it pours

Directions Read each sentence. Look at the idiom in boldface. Write an answer to the question on the line. Do *not* use the idiom in your answer.

1. Charisse was so happy that she **got off to a flying start** at her gymnastics class. What kind of start did Charisse have?

   _____

2. Hasan could hardly **keep a straight face** when he saw the mime put a rabbit on Sonya's head! What did Hasan have a hard time doing?

   _____

3. Carlotta is **in the doghouse** with her brother because she broke his CD player. What might happen to Carlotta?

   _____

4. Tonight, when Melissa gets home, she's going to have to **face the music** about why she didn't clean out her hamster's cage. What's going to happen?

   _____

5. Darnell told Jesse that it's going to be really difficult to **make ends meet** until the end of the week. What will Darnell have to do?

   _____

6. Bret said that **half a loaf is better than none** when he was offered the job of understudy for the lead actor. What does Bret mean?

   _____

7. "You and that guitar **fit like a glove**," said Ben. What does Ben mean?

   _____

8. "**Lightning never strikes twice**, so enjoy every moment of winning that trip!" Samantha's grandmother told her. Why would Samantha's grandmother say that?

   _____

9. "How long are you going to **sit on the fence** about whether you're going to try out for the baseball team?" Josh asked his friend Hari. Why did Josh ask this question?

   _____

10. Ricardo won a medal for placing first in the diving competition yesterday. Today he won a medal for placing second in the backstroke race. "**When it rains, it pours**," his mother said excitedly. What did she mean?

    _____

⭐ **Guess That Idiom** Work with a partner. Choose an idiom to illustrate, and write the idiom you're going to illustrate in your personal word journal, but don't tell your partner. On a separate paper, draw a picture that shows what the idiom means. Exchange papers with your partner, and challenge your partner to guess the idiom you illustrated.

Review and Extend

> • face the music
> • fit like a glove
> • get off to a flying start
> • half a loaf is better than none
> • in the doghouse
> • keep a straight face
> • lightning never strikes twice
> • make ends meet
> • sit on the fence
> • when it rains, it pours

BONUS IDIOMS Here are two other idioms and their meanings. Remember, you can't take the words at face value in an idiom. The expression has another meaning.

lost at sea completely confused

at the bottom of the ladder in the lowest position in a group or job

Directions Read each sentence. Then write the vocabulary or bonus idiom that best completes each sentence. You may have to change the tense of the verb in the idiom so that it fits the sentence.

1. Because Maria was new at her job as a scout for the Sea Lions, she started _____.

2. Chipper feels _____ when it comes to understanding what this new mathematics lesson is all about.

3. Derek can't stand to _____ when it comes to making decisions about his basketball career.

4. Marissa feels like she's _____ with her teammates because she only scored four points in last night's game.

5. Within the first five minutes, the Sea Lions scored a goal, and the commentator praised the team because they _____!

6. The Whalers know that they are going to have to _____ after the game because they played so poorly. The coach will not be happy. This is the fourth game the Whalers have lost.

7. The coach could not _____ when he saw Jake in the extra-large uniform that was much too big. Instead, he broke out laughing.

8. The best part of the night for the Sea Lions was that Artie scored 20 points. Artie and that basketball _____.

 Write a Sports Dialogue Work with a partner. Brainstorm some ideas for a dialogue that two sports commentators or coaches might have about a basketball or baseball game. Write the dialogue on a separate piece of paper. Use as many idioms from this lesson as you can. You may also want to use other idioms you know or have recently learned.

Check Your Mastery

Directions Read each item. Then circle the letter of the idiom that best fits the situation.

1. It was really difficult for Jasmine not to laugh when she saw her brother in that silly costume, but she didn't.
    A. face the music   **B.** keep a straight face   **C.** sit on the fence

2. Brigette had told her sister that she would be in big trouble if she even thought about borrowing her new sneakers.
    A. in the doghouse   **B.** make ends meet   **C.** when it rains, it pours

3. Joe didn't know how he would have enough money to make it through the week on his allowance. He'd spent most of it at the movies last night.
    A. face the music   **B.** get off to a flying start **C.** make ends meet

4. It really bothered Delilah that her best friend always had such a difficult time making any kind of decision.
    A. lightning never   **B.** sit on the fence   **C.** fit like a glove
    strikes twice

5. On the first day of our vacation, we went to the beach. That evening, we went to an amusement park. We were so glad that our vacation started happily.
    A. get off to a flying start   **B.** in the doghouse   **C.** face the music

6. Mark wanted to stay up late Friday and Saturday night to watch special television shows. His parents said he could only stay up late Saturday night. Mark was glad that at least he got to stay up on Saturday night.
    A. half a loaf is   **B.** sit on the fence   **C.** make ends meet
    better than none

7. Mei-ling learned to ride a horse in a very short time. Horseback riding suits her.
    A. face the music   **B.** fit like a glove   **C.** in the doghouse

8. Rodney got invitations to three different parties on the same night.
    A. lightning never   **B.** when it rains, it pours   **C.** face the music
    strikes twice

9. After Dad changed the flat tire, we continued on our trip. Dad said that we wouldn't get another flat.
    A. fit like a glove   **B.** lightning never   **C.** sit on the fence
                                    strikes twice

10. Theresa was not happy that she had to be punished for her behavior at the dinner table last night.
    A. make ends meet   **B.** get off to a flying start **C.** face the music

GLOSSARY

A

abandon (uh-**ban**-duhn) *verb*: to leave forever

absolute (**ab**-suh-loot) *adjective*: **1.** complete, total; **2.** without limit

accidentally (**ak**-si-duhnt-lee) *adverb*: in a way that is unexpected

accuse (uh-**kyooz**) *verb*: to say someone has done something wrong

additionally (uh-**dish**-uh-nuhl-lee) *adverb*: in addition to; plus; also

adjustment (uh-**juhst**-muhnt) *noun*: **1.** the act of adjusting or moving something a little bit; **2.** change

admiration (ad-**mir**-ay-*shuhn*) *noun*: **1.** the act of admiring someone or something; **2.** respect

advance (ad-**vanss**) *verb*: to move forward toward a goal

advancement (ad-**vanss**-muhnt) *noun*: the act or result of advancing or moving forward; progress

advice (ad-**vice**) *noun*: helpful information; a suggestion about what to do

advise (ad-**vize**) *verb*: to tell someone what to do

affect (uh-**fekt**) *verb*: to influence someone or something

agree (uh-**gree**) *verb*: to share the same ideas

agreement (uh-**gree**-muhnt) *noun*: a paper two people sign to say they will do something

aisle (**ile**) *noun*: the pathway between seats in a theater

almost (**awl**-most) *adverb*: very nearly

amateur (**am**-uh-chur or **am**-uh-tur) *adjective*: not professional; having to do with someone who takes part in a sport or activity for fun rather than for money

annoy (uh-**noi**) *verb*: **1.** to make someone feel angry or upset; **2.** to make someone lose patience

antique (an-**teek**) *adjective*: not new and probably valuable; old

apartment (uh-**part**-muhnt) *noun*: a set of rooms to live in within a larger building

application (ap-luh-**kay**-shuhn) *noun*: a form to fill out to apply to a job or school

aquamarine (**ak**-wuh-muh-*reen*) *noun*: **1.** a gemstone that is a blue-green color; *adjective*: **2.** the blue-green color of the sea

ascend (uh-**send**) *verb*: to go up

assume (uh-**soom**) *verb*: to suppose that something is true or will happen without checking it

aster (**ass**-tur) *noun*: a star-shaped flower with white, pink, yellow, or purple petals around a yellow center

asterisk (**ass**-tuh-risk) *noun*: a star-shaped symbol often used to indicate where something else is on a page

astronaut (**ass**-truh-*nawt*) *noun*: **1.** a traveler to the stars; **2.** someone who travels in space

astronomer (ass-**truh**-no-mur) *noun*: a scientist who studies the stars, planets, and space

astronomical (*ass*-truh-**nom**-uh-kuhl) *adjective*: **1.** having to do with the stars or their study; **2.** very large

astronomy (uh-**stron**-uh-mee) *noun*: the scientific study of the stars

at sea*: completely confused

at the bottom of the ladder*: in the lowest position in a group or job

auditorium (aw-di-**tor**-ee-uhm) *noun*: a large room where people gather for meetings, plays, concerts, and other events

available (uh-**vay**-luh-buhl) *adjective*: **1.** not busy; **2.** free to do things; **3.** ready to be used or bought

avocado (av-uh-**kah**-doh) *noun*: a green fruit with a large pit

awake (uh-**wake**) *verb*: to get up from sleep

B

bail (**bayl**) *noun*: **1.** the sum of money needed to get someone out of jail; *verb*: **2.** to empty the water out of a boat

bale (**bale**) *noun*: a bundle of something tied up tightly (hay or cotton, for example)

ballot (**bal**-uht) *noun*: **1.** a secret way of voting; **2.** a sheet of paper or a card used so a vote will be counted

banana (buh-**na**-nuh) *noun*: a yellow tropical fruit

banner (**ban**-ur) *noun*: a long piece of cloth with writing, designs, and pictures

barbecue* (**bar**-buh-kyoo) *noun*: meat cooked with a spicy sauce on an outdoor grill

barefoot (**bair**-*fut*) *adjective*: without any covering on the feet; having both feet bare

basis (**bay**-siss) *noun*: the idea or reason behind something

become (bi-**kuhm**) *verb*: to start to be

bewildered (bi-**wil**-derd) *adjective*: confused or puzzled

bite (**bite**) *verb*: **1.** to close your teeth around something; **2.** to cut with your teeth

bitter (**bit**-ur) *adjective*: **1.** upset and angry about something; **2.** very cold

blunder (**bluhn**-dur) *noun*: a foolish error; mistake

bologna (bal-**oh**-nee) *noun*: a meat named for an Italian city

bring (**bring**) *verb*: **1.** to take someone or something with you; **2.** to carry

bronze (**bronz**) *adjective*: **1.** made from a hard, brownish-gold metal; **2.** a reddish-brown color

budge (**buhj**) *verb*: to move something

c

calm (**kahm**) *adjective*: peaceful

candidate (**kan**-duh-date) *noun*: someone who is running for office in an election

capable (**keyb**-puh-buhl) *adjective*: able to do something well

carefree (**kair**-*free*) *adjective*: without any worries or cares; free from cares

careful (**kair**-fuhl) *adjective*: taking great care while doing something

carefully (**kair**-fuhl-lee) *adverb*: done in a way that shows or takes great care

carefulness (**kair**-fuhl-ness) *noun*: **1.** state or quality of being careful; **2.** giving close attention to one's work

caregiver (**kair**-*giv*-ur) *noun*: a person who gives care to sick people or who attends to the needs of a child; a doctor or nurse

careless (**kair**-luhss) *adjective*: **1.** not giving close attention to what one is doing; **2.** done without care

carelessly (**kair**-luhss-lee) *adverb*: in a way that shows little thought or care and that often leads to mistakes

carelessness (**kair**-luhss-ness) *noun*: state or quality of not being careful or not giving close attention to what one is doing

caretaker (**kair**-*tay*-kur) *noun*: a person employed to look after goods, property, or another person

caring (**kair**-ing) *adjective*: showing care or concern

carnivore (**kar**-nuh-*vor*) *noun*: a living creature that is only or mostly a meat eater

caution (**kaw**-shun) *verb*: to advise someone that something is risky or dangerous; to warn

certainly (**sur**-tuhn-lee) *adverb*: surely, definitely

channel (**chan**-uhl) *noun*: **1.** a TV or radio station; **2.** a narrow stretch of water between two pieces of land

charge (**charj**) *noun*: **1.** control or command of something; *verb*: **2.** to ask someone to pay a certain price

cheap (**cheep**) *adjective*: costing very little

cheep (**cheep**) *noun*: **1.** the sound of a baby bird; *verb*: **2.** to make a sound like a baby bird

chews (**chooz**) *verb*: grinds food with its teeth

childcare (**childe**-*kair*) *noun*: of, relating to, or providing care for children

choose (**chooz**) *verb*: to select something freely

clasp (**klasp**) *verb*: to hold somebody or something with the hands or arms; to clench

clench (**klench**) *verb*: **1.** to hold or grip tightly; to clasp; **2.** to close your teeth or fist tightly

clumsy (**kluhm**-zee) *adjective*: awkward and careless

---

* Bonus words

coffee (**kaw**-fee *or* **kof**-ee) *noun*: a hot drink made with coffee beans

cole slaw (**kohl**-*slaw*) *noun*: a side dish made with shredded cabbage

colorful (**kuhl**-ur-ful) *adjective*: **1.** full of color; **2.** having bright colors

comfortably (**kuhm**-fur-tuh-buhl-ee) *adverb*: in a relaxed way

commit (kuh-**mit**) *verb*: to do something wrong or not lawful

comparison* (kuhm-**pah**-ri-suhn) *noun*: the result of comparing two or more things

compete (kuhm-**peet**) *verb*: to try hard to do better than others at a task or in a race or other contest

condition (kuhn-**dish**-uhn) *noun*: how a person, animal, place, or thing looks or feels

connect* (kuh-**nekt**) *verb*: **1.** to link two or more things; **2.** in a test: to link ideas or to join sentences or parts of sentences

constellation (*kon*-stuh-**lay**-shuhn) *noun*: a group of stars that form a pattern in the sky

content (**kuhn**-tent) *noun*: **1.** the information in a piece of writing; what makes it up; (kon-**tent**) *adjective*: **2.** happy and satisfied

costume (**koss**-toom) *noun*: special clothes for some special purpose or event

countless (**kount**-liss) *adjective*: too many to count

craggy (**krag**-gee) *adjective*: rugged and uneven

crater (**kray**-tur) *noun*: **1.** the mouth of a volcano; **2.** the cup-shaped hole or cavity at the top of the volcano

creative (kree-**ay**-tiv) *adjective*: using or showing use of the imagination to create new ideas or things; inventive

creep (**kreep**) *verb*: to move slowly and quietly

crossroads (**krawss**-*rohdz*) *noun, plural*: **1.** the place where two roads cross one another; **2.** a point where two directions are possible

current (**kur**-uhnt) *noun*: **1.** movement of water in a river or ocean, or if electricity, in a wire; *adjective*: **2.** happening now; up-to-date

curry (**kuh**-ree) *noun*: a mixture of hot spices in a dish of meat and vegetables

custom (**kuhss**-tuhm) *noun*: **1.** something people in a certain place do, like flying the American flag on the Fourth of July; **2.** a tradition

D

damage (**dam**-ij) *verb*: to harm something

daycare (**day**-*kair*) *noun*: care given during the day to very young children away from their homes; place where care is provided

depart (di-**part**) *verb*: to leave

descend (di-**send**) *verb*: to go down

disagreeable (diss-uh-**gree**-uh-buhl) *adjective*: **1.** not pleasant; **2.** not to one's liking

discomfort (diss-**kuhm**-furt) *noun*: pain or worry

discontent (*diss*-kuhn-**tent**) *noun*: **1.** a feeling of not being satisfied; **2.** restlessness; **3.** wanting something better

discover (diss-**kuh**-vur) *verb*: to find something

displease (diss-**pleez**) *verb*: **1.** to not make someone happy or satisfied; **2.** to annoy

distinct (diss-**tingkt**) *adjective*: one of a kind

distrust (diss-**trust**) *verb*: to not trust

doctor (**dok**-tur) *noun*: a more casual way of referring to someone who treats sick people; a physician

dormant (**dor**-muhnt) *adjective*: sleeping or not active

downpour (**doun**-*por*) *noun*: heavy rains that pour down

downright (**doun**-*rite*) *adjective*: completely, totally

E

eastern (**eest**-urhn) *adjective*: in or from the east

ecosystem* (**ee**-koh-*siss*-tuhm *or* **ek**-oh-*siss*-tuhm) *noun*: a community of plants and animals that is affected by its environment, including the air, water, sunlight, and soil

effect (uh-**fekt**) *noun*: the result of a cause

election (i-**lek**-shuhn) *noun*: the act or process of choosing someone or deciding something by voting

emigrate (**em**-uh-grate) *verb*: to leave a country for good

endanger (en-**dayn**-jur) *verb*: to put in a dangerous or risky situation

endorse* (en-**dorss**) *verb*: to support or approve of someone or something

enormous (i-**nor**-muhss) *adjective*: huge

equation (i-**kway**-zhuhn *or* i-**kway**-shuhn) *noun*: a mathematical statement that one set of numbers or values is equal to another set of numbers or values

eruption (i-**rup**-shuhn) *noun*: the name for a volcano exploding

especially (ess-**pesh**-uh-lee) *adverb*: **1.** more than common; **2.** particularly

exhaust (eg-**zawst**) *verb*: to make very tired

expand (ek-**spand**) *verb*: to get larger

expect (ek-**spekt**) *verb*: to think something ought to happen

explode (ek-**splode**) *verb*: to blow apart

express* (ek-**spress**) *verb*: to show what you feel or think by saying, doing, or writing something

* Bonus words

197

extinct* (ek-**stingkt**) *adjective*: used to describe a volcano that has burned itself out and will probably not erupt in the future

extinction (ek-**stingk**-shuhn) *noun*: not existing anymore, or the state of being extinct

extreme (ek-**streem**) *adjective*: **1.** going beyond the ordinary or average; **2.** very great

F

face the music: to admit your mistake even though you may be punished

fact (**fakt**) *noun*: proven information

factors* (**fak**-tur) *noun*: one of two or more numbers that are multiplied to make a product

familiar (fuh-**mil**-yur) *adjective*: known by a lot of people

fascinate (**fass**-uh-nate) *verb*: to attract and hold someone's attention

fascination (**fass**-uh-nay-shuhn) *noun*: **1.** the act of being fascinated; **2.** being very interested in something or someone; **3.** strong interest or attraction

figurative* (**fig**-yur-uh-tiv) *adjective*: containing figures of speech such as similes, metaphors, and personification

figure of speech *noun*: an expression in which words are used in a poetic way

find (**finde**) *verb*: to discover or come across something

firm (**furm**) *noun*: **1.** a business or company; *adjective*: **2.** confident and strong

fit like a glove: a perfect fit or match

flashlight (**flash**-*lite*) *noun*: a light that you can flash on and off; a small, battery-powered lighting device

folklore (**fohk**-*lor*) *noun*: **1.** the lore, customs, stories, and beliefs of the folk, or common people; **2.** knowledge or beliefs passed from people to people

food chain (**food** *chayn*) *noun*: a chain of living beings in which smaller and weaker creatures are eaten by larger and stronger creatures

forearm (**for**-arm) *noun*: the front part of the arm

forecaster (**for**-kast-ur) *noun*: a person who tells what he or she thinks will happen in the future

foretell (for-**tel**) *verb*: **1.** to tell about something before it happens; **2.** to predict

forgive (fur-**giv**) *verb*: to pardon or to stop blaming someone

formula* (**for**-myuh-luh) *noun*: a rule that is expressed by using variables and numbers

fortunate (**for**-chuh-nit) *adjective*: lucky, favorable

fracture (**frak**-chur) *noun*: **1.** a break, split, or crack in an object or a material; *verb*: **2.** to break or shatter

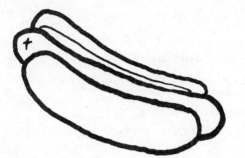

frankfurter (**frangk**-fur-tur) *noun*: a hot dog or a type of sausage

frantic (**fran**-tik) *adjective*: very upset

furious (**fyu**-ree-uhss) *adjective*: angry, fierce

G

generous (**jen**-ur-uhss) *adjective*: give or share a lot

get off to a flying start: to do well at something right from the start

glimpse (**glimps**) *verb*: to look briefly

gradually (**grad**-yoo-uhul-lee) *adverb*: **1.** slowly; **2.** bit by bit

grasp (**grasp**) *verb*: **1.** to hold something tightly; **2.** to understand

grind (**grinde**) *verb*: to crush something into a powder

guess (**gess**) *noun*: **1.** a hunch; *verb*: **2.** to form an opinion without knowing for sure

guilty (**gil**-tee) *adjective*: having done something wrong

H

half a loaf is better than none: it is better to have something rather than nothing

hamburger (**ham**-bur-gur) *noun*: a meat patty usually served on a bun

healthcare (**helth**-*kair*) *adjective*: the care given to prevent and treat illness

herbivore (**hur**-buh-*vor*) *noun*: a living creature that eats only or mostly plants

hesitate (**hez**-uh-tate) *verb*: **1.** to pause before you do something; **2.** to not do something right away

hesitation (**hez**-uh-tay-shuhn) *noun*: the act of hesitating or waiting before acting

hoarse (**horss**) *adjective*: a rough, harsh voice

holler (**hol**-lur) *verb*: to call out or shout something; to shout

horse (**horss**) *noun*: an animal that people ride

humble (**huhm**-buhl) *adjective*: unassuming in attitude and behavior; modest

hunch (**huhnch**) *noun*: an idea that is not backed by proof but comes from intuition; a guess

I

identify (eye-**den**-tuh-fye) *verb*: to tell who someone is or what something is

immense (i-**menss**) *adjective*: very large

immigrate (**im**-uh-grayt) *verb*: to come into a country to stay

impress (im-**press**) *verb*: **1.** to make someone think highly of you; **2.** to affect strongly

improve (im-**proov**) *verb*: **1.** to get better at something; **2.** to make something better

in the doghouse: to be in deep trouble

inactive* (in-**ak**-tiv) *adjective*: used to describe a volcano that is not erupting, but could erupt in the future

incredible (in-**kred**-uh-buhl) *adjective*: unbelievable or amazing

indicate (**in**-duh-kate) *verb*: to show or point out something

initial (i-**nish**-uhl) *noun*: **1.** the first letter of a name or word; *adjective*: **2.** first or at the beginning

innocent (**in**-uh-suhnt) *adjective*: not having done something wrong

insert (in-**surt**) *verb*: to add something in the right place

inspect (in-**spekt**) *verb*: to look carefully

instead (in-**sted**) *adverb*: in place of another; rather than

insult (in-**suhlt**) *verb*: to say something bad about someone

intend (in-**tend**) *verb*: to mean to do something

intention (in-**ten**-shuhn) *noun*: the act of intending or meaning to do something; a plan

inventive (in-**ven**-tiv) *adjective*: displaying creativity or imagination in its design; creative

involve (in-**volv**) *verb*: to include someone or something as a necessary part

involvement (in-**volv**-muhnt) *noun*: the act of being included or involved in some activity

is greater than (iz **grayt**-ur THan) to be more than or a larger number than; usually represented by the symbol >

is less than (iz **less** THan) to be not as much as or have fewer than; usually represented by the symbol <

isle (**eye**-uhl) *noun*: an island

issue (**ish**-oo) *noun*: topic to think about or decide on

K

kebab (**kah**-bab *or* **kee**-bab *or* **kah**-bob) *noun*: meat and vegetables on a stick

keep a straight face: able not to laugh or smile or give one's feelings away

knowledge (**nol**-ij) *noun*: information or know-how and skill

L

lava (**lah**-vuh *or* **la**-vuh) *noun*: the hot liquid that flows out of a volcano

lay* (**lay**) *verb*: **1.** to put; **2.** to place

leave (**leev**) *verb*: to go away from or out of

lie* (**lye**) *verb*: to get into or be in a flat position

lifeguard (**life**-gard) *noun*: a person who is trained to guard the life of a person who is swimming; a person trained to save swimmers in danger

* Bonus words

lighter (**lite**-ur) *noun*: **1.** a device for lighting something; *adjective*: **2.** brighter; **3.** less in weight

lightning never strikes twice: something unusual that happens once won't happen again in exactly the same way; disasters don't happen twice in a row

literal (**lit**-ur-uhl) *adjective*: meaning exactly what the words say

loose (**looss**) *adjective*: shaky; not tight; not fastened or attached firmly

loosen (**loo**-suhn) *verb*: to make something less tight

lose (**looz**) *verb*: to not have something anymore; the opposite of *find*

loudspeaker (**loud**-*spee*-kur) *noun*: a device that turns electric signals into sounds and makes the voice of the speaker loud enough to be heard over a large area

M

macaroni (mak-uh-**roh**-nee) *noun*: **1.** short, hollow tubes of pasta; **2.** a dish made from this pasta

magma (**mag**-muh) *noun*: the melted rock deep beneath the earth's surface

magnify (**mag**-nuh-fye) *verb*: **1.** to give something magnitude; **2.** to make something appear larger with, special glass

mail* (**mayl**) *noun*: letters and packages

maintain (mayn-**tayn**) *verb*: **1.** to keep something in good condition; **2.** to continue to do something

make ends meet: to be able to pay your bills

male* (**male**) *noun*: a person or animal of the sex that can father the young

manner (**man**-ur) *noun*: the way someone acts or does something

marina (muh-**reen**-ah) *noun*: **1.** a place to leave a boat; **2.** a small harbor where boats are kept

maritime (**ma**-ruh-*time*) *adjective*: having to do with ships, sailors, and the sea

masterpiece (**mass**-tur-*peess*) *noun*: a piece of work or art by a master or expert; an outstanding piece of work

memorable (**mem**-ur-uh-buhl) *adjective*: worth remembering

merely (**mihr**-lee) *adverb*: **1.** just; **2.** only; **3.** simply

metallic (muh-**tal**-ik) *adjective*: **1.** made of metal; **2.** seeming like metal

metaphor (**met**-uh-*for* or **met**-uh-*fur*) *noun*: a figure of speech in which one thing is said to be another thing

migrate (**mye**-grate) *verb*: to move from place to place, usually at fixed times

mint (**mint**) *noun*: **1.** a plant whose leaves have a strong, pleasant smell; **2.** a place where coins and bills are made

mistake (muh-**stake**) *noun*: an error or misunderstanding; blunder

* Bonus words

modern (**mod**-urn) *adjective*: **1.** up-to-date or new in style; **2.** having to do with the present

modest (**mod**-ist) *adjective*: not having or expressing a high opinion of your own achievements or abilities; humble

movement (**moov**-muhnt) *noun*: what you must have to go from one place to another

N

necessary (**ness**-uh-*ser*-ee) *adjective*: **1.** needed; **2.** important

neglect (ni-**glekt**) *verb*: to fail to take care of someone or something

nudge (**nuhj**) *verb*: to give someone or something a small push

numerous (**noo**-mur-uhss) *adjective*: more than a few things

O

occasionally (uh-**kay**-zhuh-nuhl-lee) *adverb*: from time to time

old (**ohld**) *adjective*: not new or not young; antique

omnivore (**om**-ni-vor) *noun*: a living creature that eats a wide variety of plants and animals

onward (**on**-wurd) *adverb*: forward

opinion (uh-**pin**-yuhn) *noun*: unproven information

opportunity (op-ur-**too**-nuh-tee) *noun*: a chance to do something

ordinary (**ord**-uh-*ner*-ee) *adjective*: common or everyday

P

partial (**par**-shuhl) *adjective*: not complete

passage (**pass**-ij) *noun*: a fictional or informational selection on a test

pasta (**pah**-stuh) *noun*: a noodle made of flour and water; spaghetti and macaroni are types of pasta

patient (**pay**-shuhnt) *noun*: **1.** a person treated by a doctor or other health worker; *adjective*: **2.** able to wait calmly for a result; **3.** not hasty

period (**pihr**-ee-uhd) *noun*: **1.** the punctuation mark that ends a sentence; **2.** a length of time

permanent (**pur**-muh-nuhnt) *adjective*: **1.** lasting or meant to last for a long time; **2.** not expected to change

permit (**pur**-mit) *noun*: **1.** a document giving someone the right to do something; (pur-**mit**) *verb*: **2.** to allow something

personification (**pur**-son-eh-fi-kay-shuhn) *noun*: a figure of speech in which a nonliving thing acts like a human being

physician (fuh-**zish**-uhn) *noun*: a formal word for someone trained to treat sick people; a doctor

* Bonus words

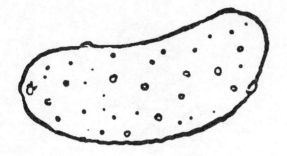

pickle (**pik**-uhl) *noun*: a cucumber soaked in salty water

plead (**pleed**) *verb*: **1.** to beg someone to do something; **2.** to say in court that you are not guilty

poetic (**poh**-eh-tik) *adjective*: like poetry; like the way a poet writes

political party (**po**-lit-uh-kuhl **par**-tee) *noun*: an organized group of people with similar beliefs who try to win elections

poll* (**pohl**) *noun*: a survey of people's opinions and beliefs

polls* (**pohlz**) *noun, plural*: the place where votes are cast and recorded during an election

powerfully (**pou**-ur-fuhl-lee) *adjective*: in a very strong way

praise (**praze**) *verb*: to say something good about someone

precede* (**pree**-seed) *verb*: to be before something or someone

predator* (**pred**-uh-tur) *noun*: an animal that lives by hunting other animals for food

prefer (**pri**-fur) *verb*: to like one thing better than another

prey (**pray**) *noun*: an animal that is hunted and eaten by another animal (or even by a meat-eating plant!)

proceed* (**pruh**-seed) *verb*: to continue or move forward

prompt (**prompt**) *noun*: a writing task outlining what is to be included in a composition

property (**prop**-ur-tee) *noun*: buildings, land, and other things belonging to someone

Q

quality (**kwahl**-uh-tee) *noun*: the fineness or worth of something

quarrel (**kwor**-uhl) *verb*: to argue

quarter (**kwor**-tur) *noun*: **1.** one of four parts; **2.** a coin representing one fourth of a dollar; *verb*: **3.** to house, to furnish with housing

R

rapid (**rap**-id) *adjective*: quick, fast

rare (**rair**) *adjective*: **1.** not often found, seen, or occurring; **2.** cooked very lightly

recently (**ree**-suhnt-lee) *adverb*: a short time ago

register (**rej**-uh-stur) *verb*: to enter your name formally so that you can vote

relation (ri-**lay**-shuhn) *noun*: **1.** a member of your family; **2.** a connection between two or more things

release (ri-**leess**) *verb*: to free something or someone

relieve (ri-**leev**) *verb*: **1.** to take away a problem or chore; **2.** to ease someone's trouble or pain

respond (ri-**spond**) *verb*: to answer a question or tell what you think about a topic

* Bonus words

restless (**rest**-liss) *adjective*: **1.** not able to keep still or to concentrate; **2.** nervous and uneasy

retreat (ri-**treet**) *noun*: **1.** a place to go to relax and think; *verb*: **2.** to move back; **3.** withdraw from a difficult situation

rise (**rize**) *verb*: **1.** to go up; **2.** to get up

root* (**root** *or* **rut**) *noun*: the underground part of a plant

route* (**root** *or* **rout**) *noun*: a road or the usual path someone or something takes

runway (**ruhn**-*way*) *noun*: **1.** a strip of ground, path, or way where aircraft seem to make a run for the sky and take off and then land; **2.** a narrow walkway on a stage

s

safeguard (**sayf**-*gard*) *noun*: **1.** something that serves as a guard or to keep things safe; *verb*: **2.** to protect someone

salsa* (**sahl**-suh) *noun*: a hot, spicy tomato sauce flavored with onions and peppers

scientific (**sye**-uhn-tif-ik) *adjective*: something that is concerned with or about science

seize (**seez**) *verb*: to grab or take hold of something quickly or suddenly

set* (**set**) *noun*: a group of numbers

shatter (**shat**-ur) *verb*: to break or cause something to break suddenly into many small, brittle pieces; to fracture

shed (**shed**) *verb*: **1.** to let something fall or drop off; **2.** to give off

shout (**shout**) *verb*: to speak in a loud or angry voice; to holler

shrink (**shringk**) *verb*: to get smaller

simile (**sim**-uh-lee) *noun*: a figure of speech in which two things are said to be similar, often using *like* or *as*

simplify (**sim**-pluh-fye) *verb*: to make something easier or simpler

sit on the fence: to not be able to make up your mind

sloppy (**slop**-ee) *adjective*: messy

sole (**sole**) *noun*: **1.** bottom part of a foot, shoe, or boot; *adjective*: **2.** only or single

spaghetti (spuh-**get**-ee) *noun*: long, thin sticks of pasta

speaker (**spee**-kur) *noun*: a person who talks before a large group of people

spectacle (**spek**-tuh-kuhl) *noun*: an exciting or remarkable sight or event

spotlight (**spot**-*lite*) *noun*: a beam of light that shines on a certain spot or area

spread (**spred**) *verb*: **1.** to cover a surface with something; **2.** to unfold or sketch out

spring (**spring**) *verb*: to jump suddenly, leap

stable (**stay**-buhl) *noun*: **1.** a building where horses or cows are kept; *adjective*: **2.** solid and steady

station (**stay**-shuhn) *noun*: a place where you go to buy tickets or receive a service

steadily (**stead**-uh-lee) *adverb*: continuously, without stopping

stellar (**stel**-uhr) *adjective*: **1.** relating to or being like a star; **2.** outstanding

strudel (**stru**-duhl) *noun*: a pastry made of dough and a sweet filling

stubborn (**stuhb**-urn) *adjective*: **1.** willful; **2.** determined

submarine (**suhb**-muh-reen *or suhb*-muh-**reen**) *noun*: a ship that can travel both on the surface of the ocean and underwater

submerge (suhb-**murj**) *verb*: to go completely underwater

subscription (suhb-**skrip**-shuhn) *noun*: a signed agreement to receive a magazine or newspaper on a regular basis

subset* (**suhb**-*set*) *noun*: part of a set

subway (**suhb**-*way*) *noun*: a train that runs under the streets of a city

subzero (**suhb**-*zihr*-oh) *adjective*: below zero

succeed (suhk-**seed**) *verb*: to get what you want

suspect (suh-**spekt**) *verb*: **1.** to think someone has done something wrong; **2.** to think something might be true

suspicious (suh-**spish**-uhss) *adjective*: distrustful, doubting

swing (**swing**) *verb*: to move back and forth, especially on a hinge

symbol (**sim**-buhl) *noun*: a sign or mark that stands for something else

T

tasty (**tayst**-ee) *adjective*: delicious

teammate (**teem**-*mate*) *noun*: a mate or fellow member of a team

tear (**tair**) *verb*: to rip or pull apart; to make an opening

terrify (**ter**-uh-fye) *verb*: **1.** to make someone feel intense fear or terror; **2.** to frighten

thunderstorm (**thuhn**-dur-*storm*) *noun*: a storm with thunder and lightning

timetable (**time**-*tay*-buhl) *noun*: a table telling the time of arrivals and departures; a schedule

tofu (**toh**-foo) *noun*: a Japanese word for bean curd

U

uncaring (**uhn**-*kair*-ing) *adjective*: **1.** having no interest or sympathy; **2.** lacking affection; **3.** without care or thought for others

uncaringly (**uhn**-*kair*-ing-lee) *adjective*: in a way that shows little care, affection, or thought for others

* Bonus words

underground (**uhn**-dur-ground) *adjective*: beneath the ground

underpay (**uhn**-dur-pay) *verb*: **1.** to pay too little for something; to pay less than something is worth

underrate (**uhn**-dur-rayt) *verb*: to value something too little

understand (*uhn*-dur-**stand**) *verb*: to know what something means or how it works

unknown (uhn-**nohn**) *adjective*: not known by anyone

unusual (uhn-**yoo**-zhoo-uhl) *adjective*: not common

usually (**yoo**-zhoo-uhl-lee) *adverb*: **1.** most of the time; **2.** normally

V

variable (**vair**-ee-uh-buhl) *noun*: a letter used to represent any one of a set of numbers

videotape (**vid**-ee-oh-*tape*) *noun*: a tape on which video or images are recorded

W

warn (**worn**) *verb*: to tell someone something about a danger or a bad thing that might happen; to caution

western (**wess**-turn) *adjective*: in or from the west

when it rains, it pours: when one thing starts to happen, everything starts to happen

INDEX